PU

SWORD O

Summoned to the Shogu_ _ _ _ _ _ _ _ _ _ _ _ _ _ _ land of Hachiman is in grave danger. The Shogun's control is slipping — some lords are breaking away and plotting treacherous deeds. Bandits roam the land freely and barbarian invaders have begun to raid across the borders. All this because the Dai-Katana, the great sword, Singing Death, has been stolen from the Shogun.

YOU are the Shogun's champion, a young Samurai. You have followed Bushido, the Way of the Warrior, and are a master of Kenjutsu, the Way of the Sword. Your mission is to recover the wondrous sword from Ikiru, the Master of Shadows, who holds it hidden deep in his mountain fastness, Onikaru, the Pit of Demons, guarded by his dreaded warrior ghosts . . .

Two dice, a pencil and an eraser are all you need to embark on this thrilling adventure of sword and sorcery. You have a choice of warrior skills — Kyujutsu, Iaijutsu, Karumijutsu or Ni-to-Kenjutsu — and your choice will affect the outcome of your mission. There are Honour points to be won and lost, too.

Many dangers lie ahead and your success is by no means certain. It's up to YOU to decide which route to follow, which dangers to risk and which adversaries to fight!

Fighting Fantasy Gamebooks

THE WARLOCK OF FIRETOP MOUNTAIN
THE CITADEL OF CHAOS
THE FOREST OF DOOM
STARSHIP TRAVELLER
CITY OF THIEVES
DEATHTRAP DUNGEON
ISLAND OF THE LIZARD KING
SCORPION SWAMP
CAVERNS OF THE SNOW WITCH
HOUSE OF HELL
TALISMAN OF DEATH
SPACE ASSASSIN
FREEWAY FIGHTER
TEMPLE OF TERROR
THE RINGS OF KETHER
SEAS OF BLOOD
APPOINTMENT WITH F.E.A.R.
REBEL PLANET
DEMONS OF THE DEEP
SWORD OF THE SAMURAI
TRIAL OF CHAMPIONS
ROBOT COMMANDO
MASKS OF MAYHEM
CREATURE OF HAVOC
BENEATH NIGHTMARE CASTLE
CRYPT OF THE SORCERER
STAR STRIDER
PHANTOMS OF FEAR
MIDNIGHT ROGUE
CHASMS OF MALICE
BATTLEBLADE WARRIOR
SLAVES OF THE ABYSS
SKY LORD
STEALER OF SOULS
DAGGERS OF DARKNESS
ARMIES OF DEATH
PORTAL OF EVIL
VAULT OF THE VAMPIRE
FANGS OF FURY

Steve Jackson's SORCERY!
1. THE SHAMUTANTI HILLS
2. KHARÉ – CITYPORT OF TRAPS
3. THE SEVEN SERPENTS
4. THE CROWN OF KINGS

FIGHTING FANTASY – *The Introductory Role-playing Game*
THE RIDDLING REAVER – *Four Thrilling Adventures*
OUT OF THE PIT – *Fighting Fantasy Monsters*
TITAN – *The Fighting Fantasy World*

Steve Jackson and Ian Livingstone present:

SWORD OF THE SAMURAI

Mark Smith and Jamie Thomson

Illustrated by Alan Langford

PUFFIN BOOKS

PUFFIN BOOKS

Published by the Penguin Group
27 Wrights Lane, London W8 5TZ, England
Viking Penguin Inc., 40 West 23rd Street, New York, New York 10010, USA
Penguin Books Australia Ltd, Ringwood, Victoria, Australia
Penguin Books Canada Ltd, 2801 John Street, Markham, Ontario, Canada L3R 1B4
Penguin Books (NZ) Ltd, 182–190 Wairau Road, Auckland 10, New Zealand

Penguin Books Ltd, Registered Offices: Harmondsworth, Middlesex, England

First published 1986
9 10 8

Concept copyright © Steve Jackson and Ian Livingstone, 1986
Text copyright © Mark Smith and Jamie Thomson, 1986
Illustrations copyright © Alan Langford, 1986
All rights reserved

Printed and bound in Great Britain by
Cox & Wyman Ltd, Reading
Typeset in 11/13pt Palatino by
Rowland Phototypesetting Ltd,
Bury St Edmunds, Suffolk

Except in the United States of America,
this book is sold subject to the condition
that it shall not, by way of trade or otherwise,
be lent, re-sold, hired out, or otherwise circulated
without the publisher's prior consent in any form of
binding or cover other than that in which it is
published and without a similar condition
including this condition being imposed
on the subsequent purchaser

CONTENTS

INTRODUCTION
7

SPECIAL RULES
14

ADVENTURE SHEET
16

BACKGROUND
18

SWORD OF THE SAMURAI
21

INTRODUCTION

Before embarking on your adventure, you must first determine your own strengths and weaknesses. You have in your possession a sword and a backpack containing Provisions (food and drink) for the trip. You are a Samurai, always prepared for any heroic mission.

To see how effective your preparations have been, you must use dice to determine your initial SKILL and STAMINA scores. On pages 16–17 there is an *Adventure Sheet* which you may use to record the details of an adventure. On it you will find boxes for recording your SKILL and STAMINA scores.

You are advised to either record your scores on the *Adventure Sheet* in pencil, or make photocopies of the page to use in future adventures.

Skill, Stamina and Luck

Roll one die. Add 6 to this number and enter this total in the SKILL box on the *Adventure Sheet*.

Roll both dice. Add 12 to the number rolled and enter this total in the STAMINA box.

There is also a LUCK box. Roll one die, add 6 to this number and enter this total in the LUCK box.

For reasons that will be explained below, SKILL, STAMINA and LUCK scores change constantly during an adventure. You must keep an accurate record of these scores and for this reason you are advised either to write small in the boxes or to keep an eraser handy. But never rub out your *Initial* scores. Although you may be awarded additional SKILL, STAMINA and LUCK points, these totals may never exceed your *Initial* scores.

Your SKILL score reflects your swordsmanship and general fighting expertise; the higher the better. Your STAMINA score reflects your general constitution, your will to survive, your determination and overall fitness; the higher your STAMINA score, the longer you will be able to survive. Your LUCK score indicates how naturally lucky a person you are. Luck – and magic – are facts of life in the fantasy kingdom you are about to explore.

Battles

You will often come across pages in the book which instruct you to fight an opponent of some sort. Battles are conducted as follows.

First record your opponent's SKILL and STAMINA scores in the first vacant Encounter Box on your *Adventure Sheet*. The scores for each opponent are given in the book each time you have an encounter.

The sequence of combat is then:

1. Roll both dice once for your opponent. Add its SKILL score. This total is your opponent's Attack Strength.
2. Roll both dice once for yourself. Add the number rolled to your current SKILL score. This total is your Attack Strength.
3. If your Attack Strength is higher than that of your opponent, you have wounded it. Proceed to step 4. If your opponent's Attack Strength is higher than yours, it has wounded you. Proceed to step 5. If both Attack Strength totals are the same, you have avoided each other's blows – start the next Attack Round from step 1 above.
4. You have wounded your opponent, so subtract 2 points from its STAMINA score. You may use your LUCK here to do additional damage (see below).
5. Your opponent has wounded you, so subtract 2 points from your own STAMINA score. Again you may use LUCK at this stage (see below).

6. Make the appropriate adjustments to either your opponent's or your own STAMINA scores (and your LUCK score if you used LUCK – see below).
7. Begin the next Attack Round by repeating steps 1–6. This sequence continues until the STAMINA score of either you or your opponent has been reduced to zero (death).

Fighting More Than One Opponent

Sometimes you will find yourself under attack from more than one person or creature. When this happens, each will make a separate attack on you in each Attack Round, but you must choose which one you will fight. Attack your chosen target as in normal battle. Against the other, you must throw for your Attack Strength in the normal way, but even if your Attack Strength is greater you will not inflict a wound. Just count this as though you have parried an incoming blow. However, if your Attack Strength is lower, you will have been wounded in the normal way.

Luck

At various times during your adventure, either in battles or when you come across situations in which you could either be lucky or unlucky (details of these are given on the pages themselves), you may call on your LUCK to make the outcome more favourable. But beware! Using LUCK is a risky business and if you are *un*lucky, the results could be disastrous.

The procedure for using your LUCK is as follows: roll two dice. If the number rolled is equal to or less than your current LUCK score, you have been lucky and the result will go in your favour. If the number rolled is higher than your current LUCK score, you have been unlucky and you will be penalized.

This procedure is known as *Testing your Luck*. Each time you *Test your Luck*, you must subtract 1 point from your current LUCK score. Thus you will soon realize that the more you rely on your LUCK, the more risky this will become.

Using Luck in Battles

On certain pages of the book you will be told to *Test your Luck* and will be told the consequences of your being lucky or unlucky. However, in battles, you always have the option of using your LUCK either to inflict a more serious wound on an opponent you have just wounded, or to minimize the effects of a wound your opponent has just inflicted on you.

If you have just wounded your opponent, you may *Test your Luck* as described above. If you are Lucky, you have inflicted a severe wound and may subtract an *extra* 2 points from your opponent's STAMINA score. However, if you are Unlucky, the wound was a mere graze and you must restore 1 point to your opponent's STAMINA (i.e. instead of scoring the normal 2 points of damage, you have now scored only 1).

If your opponent has just wounded you, you may *Test your Luck* to try to minimize the wound. If you are Lucky, you have managed to avoid the full damage of the blow. Restore 1 point of STAMINA (i.e. instead of doing 2 points of damage it has done only 1). If you are Unlucky, you have taken a more serious blow. Subtract 1 extra STAMINA point.

Remember that you must subtract 1 point from your own LUCK score each time you *Test your Luck*.

Restoring Skill, Stamina and Luck

Skill

Your SKILL score will not change much during your adventure. Occasionally, a page may give instructions to increase or decrease your SKILL score.

Stamina and Provisions

Your STAMINA score will change a lot during your adventure as you fight and undertake arduous tasks. As you near your goal, your STAMINA level may be dangerously low and battles may be particularly risky, so be careful!

Your backpack contains enough Provisions for ten meals. You may rest and eat at any time except when engaged in a battle. The text will not tell you when you can do this: it is up to you. Eating a meal restores 4 STAMINA points. When you eat a meal, add 4 points to your STAMINA score and deduct 1 point from your Provisions. A separate Provisions Remaining box is provided on the *Adventure Sheet* for recording details of Provisions. Remember that you have a long way to go, so use your Provisions wisely!

Luck

Additions to your LUCK score are awarded through the adventure when you have been particularly lucky. Details are given on the pages of the book. Remember that, as with SKILL and STAMINA, your LUCK score may never exceed its *Initial* value, unless specially instructed by the text.

SPECIAL RULES

As a Samurai, there are certain skills at which you may be expert. Depending on which skill you choose, you will be told in the text when you can use it, or else the skill will effect combat in some way. Choose *one* skill from the following list.

Kyujutsu (Archery)

This skill allows you to start with the Samurai bow and a set of twelve arrows, consisting of three willow-leaf arrows (2 STAMINA damage), three bowel-rakers (3 STAMINA damage), three armour-piercers (2 STAMINA damage, but required for use against certain opponents) and three humming bulbs (1 STAMINA damage, but makes a frightening noise). You must keep a record of the number and type of your arrows on your *Adventure Sheet*. When you are asked if you wish to fire an arrow, choose the arrow you wish to use and cross it off your list. Sometimes you may be lucky enough to regain an arrow or find some more. To see whether or not you hit a target, you will have to roll a number on two dice less than your SKILL. You will be told when to use an armour-piercer or a humming bulb.

Iaijutsu (Fast draw)

This skill enables you to draw your sword and strike all in one fast motion. This means that you will always hit your enemy, no matter what his SKILL rating, *in the first round of combat only*, doing 3 STAMINA points of damage.

Karumijutsu (Heroic leaping)

This enables you to make fantastic leaps and acrobatic jumps. You will be told when you can use this.

Ni-to-Kenjutsu

This is the skill of fighting with two swords, the wakizashi (shortsword) and the katana (longsword). All Samurai carry both swords, but not all have this special skill at using them simultaneously. With this skill, if you attack an opponent and roll 9 or more, you may make another attack, before your enemy has the chance to fight back. (If you roll 9 or more on your second throw you *cannot* have yet another attack!)

Honour Points

As a Samurai of the Shogun of Hachiman, you are bound by giri (duty) and Honour. You begin the adventure with 3 Honour points. Certain actions will increase Honour, others reduce it. If your Honour is ever reduced to 0, turn to paragraph **99**, no matter what you are doing at the time. Also, your Honour will have a bearing on whether or not you can do certain things in the adventure.

ADVENTURE SHEET

SKILL	STAMINA	LUCK
Initial Skill= 10	*Initial Stamina=*	*Initial Luck=* 10

NOTES

HONOUR
8

PROVISIONS REMAINING
Katana
Wakizashi

SPECIAL SKILL

BACKGROUND

The world of Titan has three main continents – Allansia, Khakabad and Khul, the Dark Continent. It is on the eastern coast of Khul that the land of Hachiman lies; the sea on one side and mountains on all the others cut Hachiman off from the rest of the continent.

The capital of Hachiman is Konichi and its ruler is Kihei Hasekawa, the Shogun. You are a young Samurai, the Shogun's champion, and said by many to be Kensei or 'Sword Saint'. You have faithfully followed Bushido, the Way of the Warrior, and are a master of Kenjutsu, the Way of the Sword.

One day the Shogun summons you to his presence and tells you a dreadful tale:

'Hachiman is in grave danger. My control is slipping – some lords are seeking to break away and declare their estates independent; others have already done so, and plot against me. Bandits roam the land freely and barbarian invaders have begun to raid across our borders, knowing that Hachiman is weak. All this because the Dai-Katana, the great sword Singing Death, has been stolen from me.'

Singing Death is a wondrous sword, said to bestow great powers on its keeper, and to be the soul of Hachiman. 'He who wields Singing Death and uncovers the secret of the sword will rule Hachiman,' the Shogun continues. 'Many lords say I now have no right to rule; some seek to take the sword for themselves, others have already changed their allegiance to he who now holds the sword. And no keeper could be worse: it is Ikiru, Master of Shadows, that soulless dog who cowers in his mountain fastness, Onikaru, the Pit of Demons. Now that he has the sword, Bakemono-Sho and Shikome are flocking to his banners, and he summons forth Shura, warrior ghosts, from the pit to aid him. Soon, if he uncovers the secret of the sword, he will overrun our beautiful land of cherry blossoms.

'You have senki, war spirit, and to you I entrust this mission. Go, my champion, to Onikaru, slay Ikiru and bring me Singing Death. It will not be easy. To slay Ikiru and to defeat his infernal allies you will have to uncover the secret of Singing Death. I cannot tell you the secret, for it is written that he who freely reveals it will be damned for ever to the nether regions, and Singing Death will disappear from the world of men. You will have to solve the puzzle yourself. I will pray to the Kami of the Heavens for your success, and may Hotei god of luck smile on you. Here, take this, the Seal of the Shogun. It will give you safe passage through those areas still loyal to me.'

Turn to **1**.

1

You gather your weapons, your katana (longsword) and wakizashi (shortsword), your battle armour and Provisions. The guards salute you as you leave the main gate of Konichi. You follow the road north through the beautiful countryside surrounding the capital; soon you come to a fork in the road. Will you go west and north, to the Forest of Shadows, Hagakure Bridge and on to the Shios'ii Mountains (turn to **10**), or east, to the ford, through the Mizokumo Fens and thence to the mountains (turn to **29**)?

2

'Well, man-thing, here is the first riddle:

In marble halls as white as milk,
Lined with a skin as soft as silk,
Within a fountain crystal-clear,
A golden apple doth appear;
No doors are there to this stronghold
Yet thieves break in and steal the gold.'

The Tatsu stares at you in greedy anticipation. When you think you have the answer, take each letter of the answer (don't count words such as 'a' or

'the'), convert it to its corresponding number in the alphabet (i.e. a number from 1 to 26), add them together and turn to that paragraph number.

So, if the answer was 'fire' (which it isn't!), you would turn to 38.

$$F \quad I \quad R \quad E$$
$$6 + 9 + 18 + 5 = 38$$

If the paragraph you turn to is the wrong one (it won't make sense!), turn to **26**.

3

The yellow eyes of the nearest monster show a gleam of intelligence as you bow in surrender. It reaches for your sword, which you decide to give it, since you still have your shorter wakizashi. The monster then motions you to cross over the ford. Your katana is the sword with which you are most skilful. Subtract 1 from your SKILL until you find another katana, or Singing Death itself. You cross the ford. Turn to **245**.

4

You hurtle down the stairs as fast as you can. You can hear the guards behind you, but their footfalls stop at the top of the stairs. A laugh echoes down the stairs, as does the voice of another: 'We shall never see that one again. The Mukade will see to that!' You run on, knowing you cannot go back: you will have to face whatever lies ahead. At the bottom of the stairs a dank, rough-cut tunnel runs into blackness ahead. *Test your Luck*. If you are Lucky, turn to **16**. If you are Unlucky, turn to **38**.

5

Suspicious of whatever caused the old charcoal-burner's death, you skirt the perimeter of the village, but all looks normal and peaceful. Peasants go about their business, mostly returning home as dusk falls. Some of the older villagers are gathering outside the headman's house. Will you ask one of the peasants for hospitality (turn to **71**), or join the elders at the headman's house (turn to **319**)?

6

It is an easy matter to bury yourself in the hay without the driver noticing. Soon you can hear the guards questioning him and then the sound of the great oak doors rumbling open. *Test your Luck*. If you are Lucky, turn to **14**. If you are Unlucky, turn to **28**.

7

Shielding your head with your wakizashi, you give ground as a storm of flaming brands sizzle through the air. One catches on the fastening of your lacquered armour, burning you badly (lose 2 STAMINA points). If you are still alive, you utter a blood-curdling cry of rage and lop off the fire-wielder's head with one clean sweep of your katana. You charge the rest, but they scatter into the woods. You beat out the flames that are threatening to consume

you. You have defended the Shogun's honour and you may add 1 to your own Honour score before continuing on your way. Turn to **195**.

8

You are slowly working your way up the mountainside when a tingling sensation, like an itch on your brain, causes you to pull up short. You look up, and suddenly an imposing figure stands before you. Dressed in fine robes and armour of silver and gold, it is a tall, muscular man-like being. Its face is handsome to look upon, clean and pure; but it is the purity of complete evil. Its eyes burn with violet flame and its whole being radiates power and malice. It is a Dai-Oni, or greater demon.

'So, mortal, you would seek entry to the domain of Ikiru, Master of Shadows?' it says, its words resonant with strength. 'To do so, you must defeat me in the Tourney of the Planes.' Then the Dai-Oni begins to fade, laughing maniacally, the laughter echoing like thunder all around you.

Suddenly you find yourself in open space. In every direction stretch the endless stars, and your mind reels as you try to take it all in. Then your vision fixes on the doors, bringing you back from the edge of madness. You are surrounded by eight doors, one in each of the walls of an octagonal room; but the walls, ceiling and floor are transparent.

Then the voice of the Dai-Oni fills your head. 'This place is called the Hub. Behind each door lies some powerful beast. You must try to win as many of these creatures over to your cause as you can. They will then aid you in battle. For, when you are ready, you will have to face me and my allies in a struggle to the death at the Place of Battle. If, somehow, you should triumph, then you may enter the Pit of Demons and there meet your fate at the hands of Ikiru. So let it begin, and may fortune desert you and the blight of a thousand sores be visited upon you.' The voice fades. It seems you have no choice but to play the Tourney of the Planes. Each door is labelled. Which door will you go through first:

The Pinnacle of Ultimate Height?	Turn to **30**
The Elder Plains?	Turn to **68**
The Mountain of Ineffable Holiness?	Turn to **66**
The Endless Sands of Akhon?	Turn to **78**
The Swamps of Primordial Mire?	Turn to **98**
The Eternal Tower?	Turn to **110**
The Enchanted Wood?	Turn to **126**
The Place of Battle?	Turn to **138**

9

Flailing wildly, you fight your way to the village's edge and then run into the darkness. The Rokuro-Kubi that remain intact after the savage beating inflicted on them decide to let you go. You have survived the Village of the Undead. Add 1 to your LUCK and turn to **397**.

10

You journey on through the lands of Hachiman. Wherever you pass, people bow with respect, recognizing either the Shogun's champion or the Shogun's seal. This close to Konichi the land is as it ever was, peaceful and happy. After a few days, habitations become more sparse. You are travelling through the domain of Lord Tsietsin when you notice a plume of smoke on the horizon. As you draw near, you can see it is a burning village. You shake your head sorrowfully at the state Hachiman is in, when raiders can strike into the heart of one of the lords' territories. A dusty track leads from the road to the village. Will you investigate the village (turn to **34**), or decide your mission is too important and press on (turn to **24**)?

11

You tell the elders that you have left some belongings outside the village and that you will return with them shortly, but they seem unwilling to let you go. You end up forcing your way past them and walking behind some houses to avoid their prying eyes. When out of sight you make for the village's end. Turn to **15**.

12

'So,' the Tatsu thunders, 'you have managed to get as far as the Tourney of the Planes, mortal! Well done! I have decided to help you in your battle against the Dai-Oni, for I too wish to see Ikiru, Master of Shadows, slain. When you step through the portal to the Place of Battle, I shall be there to fight for you.' With that it flies away. You can do nothing more, so you step back through the door behind you, and find yourself back at the Hub, surrounded by stars. Note down that you have won over the Tatsu to your cause before returning to **8** and choosing another option. Do not choose an option you have already tried.

13

Three of the scaly green monsters attack you at once, rushing the mound to try to sweep you off it with their webbed claws. You must give battle.

	SKILL	STAMINA
First KAPPA	8	14
Second KAPPA	8	12
Third KAPPA	7	13

If you reduce one of the Kappa to 4 STAMINA points or less, turn to **31**.

14

The cart is driven into the stable. The driver stomps away, muttering something about a parched throat after a long journey, and you quietly climb down to the stable floor. Across the castle courtyard is a square stone keep, with pagoda-like roofs and carved gables, the palace of Lord Tsietsin. But it is the two palace guards flanking the doors that really draw your attention. They are Shikome, vile humanoid beings, but hairy as apes, and with claws, fangs and horrible snouted faces. They are dressed in dirty and tattered imitations of Samurai armour, although their weapons seem in excellent condition. The presence of Shikome can only mean that Tsietsin is in league with Ikiru, Master of Shadows. Tsietsin will be in the palace, and it seems even more important than before to slay him.

When it is late evening, you decide to act. If you have the skill of Kyujutsu, you can try to kill both the guards as swiftly as possible with two single bow-shots (turn to **46**). If you cannot, or do not wish to use this skill, you can walk casually towards them and then suddenly attack (turn to **64**), walk forward and say you have an important message for Lord Tsietsin (turn to **84**), or simply stride forward as authoritatively as possible, salute and walk into the palace as if they were not there (turn to **100**).

15

You head hastily in the opposite direction to that by which you entered the village. Nobody appears to notice you leave and you begin to breathe easier – there was something unnatural about the villagers. Suddenly you catch sight of the old charcoal-burner who brought you to the village. You thought him quite dead, having left his unbreathing corpse at the other edge of the village, yet here he is grinning at you from behind a wall. You step forward, unable to believe your eyes – but then stop as his head sails up into the night air. It has completely detached itself from his body. With a thrill of horror you realize that this is an undead being, a Rokuro-Kubi, whose heads detach themselves at night in order to hunt. It spits black gobbets of poison which hiss and smoke as they spatter against your face. You are in agony. Lose 2 STAMINA points. You must fight the Rokuro-Kubi as it flies through the air snapping viciously.

ROKURO-KUBI   SKILL 7   STAMINA 8

If you win, turn to **153**.

16

There is a sudden crack, as loud as thunder, and a rusted iron portcullis slams down behind you, where you had been an instant ago. There is no return now in any case, and you press on. A fetid odour reaches your nostrils and, up ahead, a milky luminescence glows as you draw near. Turn to **50**.

17

The journey to the Spider Fens across open lawless territory takes three days, during which you take the bare minimum of rest, not wishing to be caught out in the open by mounted Samurai in the service of Ikiru, Master of Shadows. The air seems unnaturally chill as you enter the dreaded Spider Fens, but you console yourself with the thought that taking this route will allow you to penetrate deep within Ikiru's territory before he knows of your presence. A paved road stretches into the delta, running north in the right direction for you. It runs on a dyke surrounded by lakes and marshes on either side. At last the fog comes down and you can see no further than a few cracked flagstones ahead. At length you come to a junction. The paved road veers north-east into the fog. A well-trodden path leads north past a signpost saying 'The Well of Souls', and another dyke leads along the edge of a mist-covered lake to the west. If you have a map showing the route to a scarlet pagoda, turn to **107**. If not, will you head north (turn to **285**), west (turn to **125**) or north-east (turn to **249**)?

18

You race up the stairs and burst into a small guard-room. A single soldier stares at you in surprise. You dart past him into the corridors of the palace, but the alarm has been raised now. You lead them a merry chase, but there is no escape from Tsietsin's castle, not with all his men after you. At last you are caught and, although you fight bravely, you are overwhelmed and hacked into pieces.

19

The Tatsu seems disappointed. 'An egg. Yes, that is right, man-thing.' Then it brightens, the look of greed coming back into its eyes. 'But can you succeed again, sharp-witted mortal?

> When one does not know what it is,
> Then it is something;
> But when one knows what it is,
> Then it is nothing.'

Again, when you think you have the answer, take each letter of the answer, convert it to its corresponding number in the alphabet, add them together and turn to that paragraph number. If the paragraph you turn to is the wrong one, turn to **26**.

20

The gaoler utters a grunt of annoyance. *Test your Luck*. If you are Lucky, turn to **282**. If you are Unlucky, turn to **296**.

21

The humming-bulb arrow speeds to its mark in the chest of one of the monsters, but the whining shriek it makes as it flies through the air has no effect on them. The other rakes you with a webbed claw, then body-checks you as you struggle away from the frothing white water at the edge of the pier of rock. Lose 3 STAMINA points. You are sent slipping and sliding to the very brink of disaster as it moves in to attack again. You cannot find your balance, and so you decide to commit yourself to the hidden mystery of the frothing white water below the ford. Turn to **49**.

22

Eleanor steps forward and unleashes a crackling bolt of blue energy from her hands. It strikes Gargantus in the face and his ruby eyes explode like coloured glass. Gargantus utters a thunderous roar of pain, before toppling to the ground, inert, merely a statue of bronze now.

Eleanor turns to you and says. 'I have paid my debt to you now, and must leave. Good luck, warrior.' She gestures and fades away, back to wherever she came from.

The Dai-Oni speaks: 'You have done well, mortal, but now I shall kill you.' It advances, wielding a massive spiked iron club, a Tetsubo. If you still have the Ki-Rin as an ally, you may send it against the Dai-Oni (turn to **394**). Otherwise, you will have to fight the Dai-Oni alone (turn to **292**).

23

Shielding your head with your wakizashi, you give ground as a storm of flaming brands sizzle through the air. One catches in the fastening of your lacquered armour and another dislodges your helmet. You are burnt badly and almost concussed (lose 5 STAMINA points). If you are still alive, you give vent to a blood-curdling cry of rage and lop off the fire-wielder's head with one clean sweep of your

katana. You charge the rest, but they scatter into the woods; you stop to beat out the flames that are threatening to consume you. You have defended the Shogun's honour and you may add 1 to your own Honour score before continuing on your way. Turn to **195**.

24

You walk on. Soon the village fades from view as you pass through the rolling fields of farmlands. The main road curves past a low hill, and when you round it, you see a fortified castle some way from the road. You recognize the flag of Lord Tsietsin, the local daimyo or baron, fluttering above the towered ramparts. If you have already met some of Lord Tsietsin's men, turn to **314**. If you have not, turn to **326**.

25

You sink twenty feet below the chill surface of the pool beneath the well, weighed down by your lacquered armour. You might just be able to surface with your swords if you can struggle out of your armour in time, but your lungs are already bursting. If your current STAMINA is 12 or less, turn to **353**; if it is more than 12, turn to **313**.

26

'No, man-thing, that is incorrect,' the Tatsu says greedily, its eyes glowing with baleful fire. 'And now I shall devour you!' It roars and launches itself at you, jaws snapping horribly. You must fight it.

TATSU SKILL 11 STAMINA 13

If you win, turn to **42**.

27

Somewhere within you, you find the strength to resist the evil blandishments of Ikiru's demon. When you do so it abruptly disappears. There is a hiss of indrawn breath as Ikiru starts in rage.

'You dare to resist me, petty mortal,' he croaks. Before you can run forward to try to grab Singing Death, Ikiru rises from his throne and rushes at you – in fact, he floats across the ground. His hands are talons of black nothingness. You ready yourself for combat, but before he reaches you, Ikiru spreads his arms and bolts of black energy leap from his arms to engulf you. You are cursed, charred and crippled all at once. Lose 2 LUCK points, 4 STAMINA points and 2 SKILL points. If you still live, a sword of black steel, etched with glowing red runes appears in his hands and he swings at you, his face a mask of shadow, dark and featureless. You must fight him.

IKIRU   SKILL 12   STAMINA 12

Each time Ikiru hits you and you remain alive, *Test your Luck*. If you are Lucky, fight on. If you are Unlucky, turn to **109**. If you manage to defeat him, turn to **400**.

28

Suddenly there is a shout of 'Ho, what's this? A foot in the hay!' and a burst of laughter. The hay is ripped away and several Samurai guards are levelling their spears at you. 'So, the Shogun's champion skulks in the hay like a common pig-herder!' says a cruel-looking man in a kimono. 'I am Ieratsu, Lord Tsietsin's lieutenant. We welcome you to his castle,' he says wryly. Then he signals and the guards leap upon you. You struggle, but there are too many of them and soon you have been overpowered.

You are unceremoniously thrown into a small cell in the palace dungeon. The gaoler, a large beefy man in a stained leather jerkin, says jeeringly, 'You will be taken before the Shogun Tsietsin on the morrow.' He then slams the massive, iron-studded, oaken door of the cell in your face.

You are alone. They have taken your swords, and it

is this rather than the cruel gibes and the indignity of capture that fills you with shame. Lose 1 Honour point for their loss. There is nothing you can do but wait for the morning, so you lie down on the wooden pallet in the corner and go to sleep. Turn to **316**.

29

The east road which meanders across the plain of the great Hang-Yo river bustles with activity. Here in the fertile river valley, swept constantly by the Shogun's Samurai patrols, many of the people

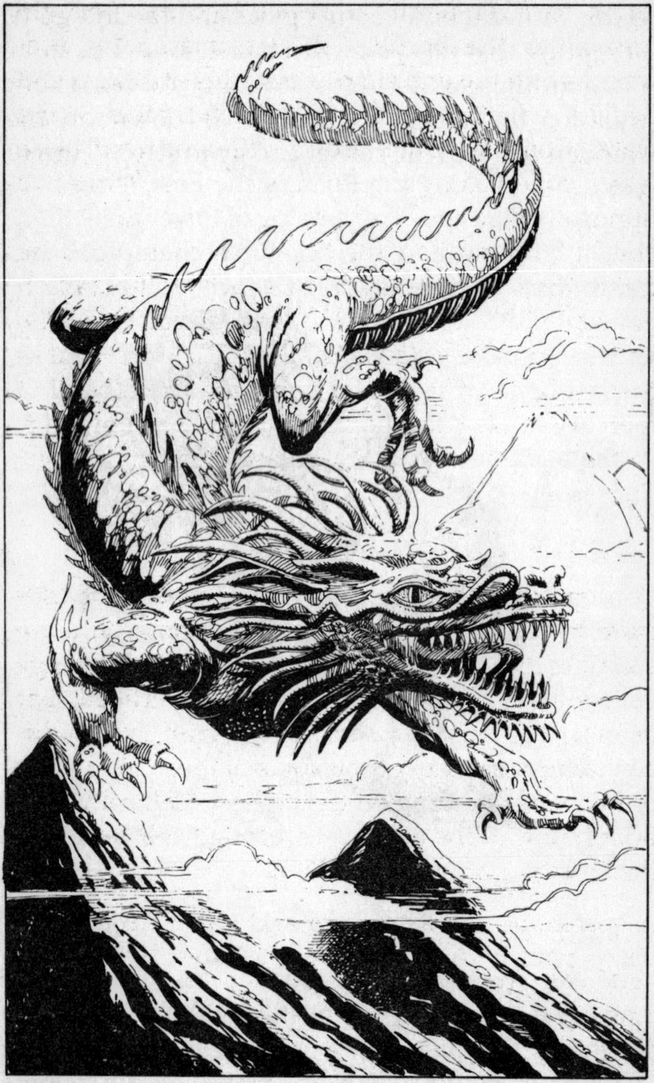

know nothing of the unrest which has brought turmoil to the borders of Hachiman. The rice-wagons and the impromptu caravans of tinkers and pedlars which pass along the road plying their wares from fief to fief are no different from those which rolled along the Road of the East Wind two hundred years ago. They, being of lower caste than you, a Samurai and the Shogun's champion, are careful that the wheels of their carts do not splash your splendid armour, and all bow as you pass. The journey into the uplands is peaceful enough, but as the last bend of the river, twinkling like a band of mercury in the late afternoon sun, falls out of sight, so the attitude of the peasants you meet changes. Turn to **43**.

30

You open the door marked 'The Pinnacle of Ultimate Height'. The next thing you know, you are standing on a thin pinnacle of rock, high in a strange yellow sky. An orange sun burns overhead. Far below, the ground is a dark red colour. From horizon to horizon tower thousands of these pinnacles, but you are standing on the highest. Behind you, a door hangs in the air, a gate through the worlds to the Hub.

A speck appears in the sky and grows larger as it nears you. It turns out to be a Tatsu, a wingless air-riding dragon. It has a massive serpent-like body, with four taloned legs, and it seems to be walking on air. If you have encountered the Tatsu in the Forest of Shadows already, turn to **144**. If not, turn to **156**.

31

The scaly green flesh of the monsters turns a dull purplish colour where your sword strikes, until their flesh looks like rotting fruit, but the wounds don't seem to be affecting them as much as you would expect. Other green figures lumber out of the water to take the place of those you have been fighting and you will soon be surrounded. You may not be able to defeat these creatures through swordsmanship alone. Turn to **41**.

32

The undead warrior fights in eerie silence. Your last blow shatters one of its skeletal arms and it executes another leap, which takes it out of range.

Suddenly, it turns virtually invisible, until only a reddish outline enables you to determine its position. Then it attacks you again. Continue the fight, but you cannot use Iaijutsu again if you have that skill, and subtract 2 from your skill while it is invisible. The first time you hit it, turn to **58**.

33

As you approach the estuary through the mire of the fens, it begins to rain. You slog on, but the rainfall is torrential and you are soon soaked through and bespattered with mud from head to foot. It rains for two days, by which time you decide to turn back. The water-level rises until you are forced to swim. After several miles you drown, utterly exhausted.

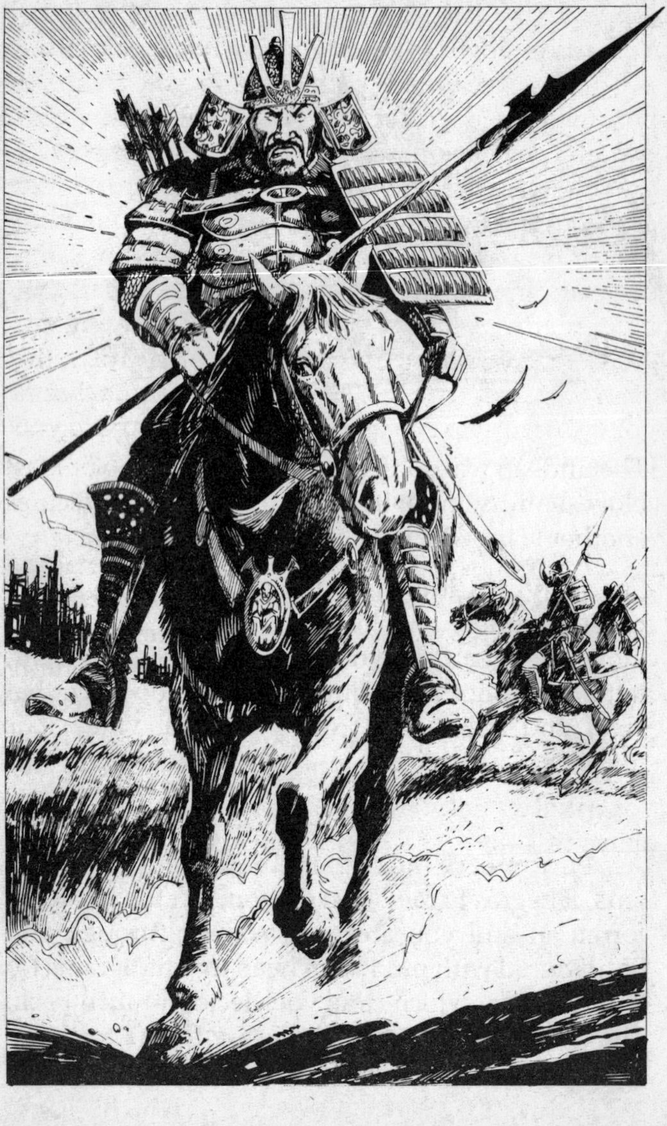

34

You stride down the dusty track, but break into a run when screams of pain come to you from the burning village. You can see horsemen, presumably bandits, charging in among the fleeing villagers. A grove of trees obscures your view for a moment, and as you round it, a horseman gallops up the trail from the village towards you. It is a Samurai, with a long spear in one hand, and dressed in the green and blue lacquered armour of Tsietsin, the lord of this area. Will you run towards him, show him the Shogun's seal, and order him to tell you what is going on (turn to **44**), or wait for him to come to you (turn to **56**)?

35

As three of the green monsters rush the mound, hoping to sweep you off it, you launch yourself into a great leap that carries you towards the tree-tops. You hurtle above the monsters and land behind them. They turn and run towards you. You have only two choices: to run (turn to **173**) or to place your back against a tree and fight (turn to **183**). However, you noticed something of interest as you sailed above their heads. The flat-topped heads are in fact basins, each holding a small pool of water. The balancing act which they appear to be doing is in order to keep the water inside their basin heads.

36

The Phoenix's eyes dull and its flames flicker and go out. It falls before you, all life expunged. But then, suddenly, it erupts into flame once more, but this time it is consumed in the fire until only ashes remain.

Then, incredibly, another Phoenix, smaller this time, bursts out of the ashes; it pauses in the air to give a scream of exultation before taking to the skies and disappearing (to your relief). Amazed at what you have seen, you stand in thought for a moment, before turning round and leaving through the door. You find yourself back at the Hub. Return to **8** and choose again, but you cannot choose an option you have tried already.

37

Mustering as much authority as you can in the unfortunate circumstances, you order the peasants to free you from the trap. One by one the charcoal-burners approach, wary that you may be tricking them; when they see your plight they grin unpleasantly and discuss what they are going to do with the trapped Samurai. The most popular idea is to bury you alive inside one of the charcoal ovens. They strip bark from a nearby tree preparatory to binding you. Will you tell them of the importance of your mission (turn to **89**), or warn them that they will be haunted by spirits if they kill the Shogun's champion (turn to **101**)?

38

There is a sudden crash, as loud as thunder, and you are racked with a surge of pain as something slams into your back, sending you sprawling. Lose 3 STAMINA points. If you still live, a rusted iron portcullis has crashed down behind you, sealing off any hope of return. You press on. A fetid odour reaches your nostrils and, up ahead, a milky luminescence glows as you draw near. Turn to **50**.

39

Your lungs have been pierced by the three barbed tines of the trident. You fall to the floor, coughing blood. You have fallen into the hands of the Kappa, from which there is no escape. They drag you into the gloomy depths of the river, even as you die.

40

The gaoler moves on, waking other prisoners, sliding black bread and stale water through flaps in the doors. Presently he returns and opens your cell door. But this time he has three soldiers with him. Will you pretend to have been wounded and then suddenly attack them (turn to **370**), or pretend to have been wounded and when they have taken you out of the cell, grab a weapon and try to run away (turn to **380**)?

41

If you have the skill of Karumijutsu and wish to use it to leap over the heads of your assailants, turn to **35**. Otherwise, you find yourself forced on to the defensive by their powerful attacks. Your sword flashes through the air as if a magical barrier of blades surrounded you, but your foes press in on all sides. At last, one gets through your guard, and rakes you with its claws. Lose 2 STAMINA points. If you are still alive, turn to **129**.

42

The dragon rolls over and dies. Then, incredibly, it fades out of existence before your very eyes, as if it had never been. Around you the forest loses the aura of mystery and magic that seemed to enclose it. You press on, following the track on the other side of the clearing. Turn to **82**.

43

The deference normally accorded to one of your standing in society is sadly missing in the behaviour of the first uplanders you meet. They are charcoal-burners, grimed grey with the soot of their trade. One of them, younger than the others, recognizes the standard that flaps in the wind behind your back and scorns you: 'Look, friends, it is the rightful champion of the wrongful king. Where is your master's sword? Where is your master, without the sword? Hasekawa, bless his shaven pate, is no Shogun. You have no master, you are ronin.' Ronin are Samurai who have no lord and have lost their status. The peasant is insulting you and the Shogun. The other charcoal-burners shout at the youngster to be quiet. Will you punish the youth (turn to **59**), or walk on as if you hadn't noticed (turn to **77**)?

44

You call out, in the name of Kihei Hasekawa, and ask the Samurai rider what is going on. He canters towards you, saying, 'Bandit raiders! I am riding now for the fort of Lord Tsietsin.' Suddenly, as he nears you, he levels his spear and spurs his horse on, catching you completely by surprise, and gashing your arm. Lose 3 STAMINA points. You must fight the treacherous Samurai.

SAMURAI HORSEMAN   SKILL 8   STAMINA 9

If you win, turn to **72**.

45

You manage to keep going towards the edge of the village and are confronted by the flimsy wall of one of the small houses. Putting your head down you burst through the wall and out through the other side, gaining time on the heads as as they sail over the roof. Only a few heads await you at the village's edge. You must give battle again.

ROKURO-KUBI   SKILL 8   STAMINA 8

If you win, turn to **9**.

46

Notching a bowel-raker to your bow, you take careful aim and prepare to kill the Shikome guards as fast as you can. Roll two dice. If the result is less than your SKILL, turn to **236**. If it is equal to or greater than your SKILL, turn to **248**.

47

The power of the black runesword drains your vital life force: Lose 1 SKILL and 1 LUCK point. Return to **199** and fight on.

48

She stares at you quizzically. What item will you try to use:

A horn?	Turn to **86**
A Potion of Waters of Knowledge?	Turn to **96**
A Helmet of Befuddlement?	Turn to **114**

If you have none of these, turn to **130**.

49

You cast yourself down into the frothing whiteness of the river, only to find, to your horror, that the monsters have concealed sharpened stakes just below the surface, upon which you have impaled yourself. Lose 7 STAMINA points. If you are still alive, you painfully drag yourself off the stakes, which have punctured your flesh in several places, and are washed up on the far bank. Turn to **395**.

The smell grows stronger. You come out into a large cavern, suffused with a sickly pale light, but the source of the light is for the moment indiscernible. Bones, old clothes and rusted weapons are strewn about. Then you spot it. A huge glowing shape comes towards you. An enormous gaping maw, lined with teeth, rises up to devour you. Two eyes, massive discs of inscrutable blackness, stare at you, alive with ancient evil. The body, supported by hundreds of black scuttling legs, is bony and segmented. It is a dirty white colour and it is this that gives off the pale glow. It is a Mukade, some sort of gigantic, forty-foot centipede. It ripples towards you, intent on making you its next meal. If you have the skill of Kyujutsu, and still have your bow and arrow, you may fire two arrows before it is upon you. (You will not be able to reclaim the arrows if you win the fight.)

MUKADE   SKILL 7   STAMINA 20

If you win, turn to **62**.

51

You watch as Ikiru summons more shadow beings to him. Then he waves and they rush to attack you, each an amorphous mass of blackness, which tries to engulf you. You must fight ten of these creatures in a row, one by one. However, each time you hit one, Singing Death pulses with light and destroys it utterly. Each of the ten Shadows has SKILL 9, STAMINA 1. If you slay all ten, you skirt the pit and confront Ikiru, face to empty black face. Turn to **121**.

52

The Tatsu stiffens in surprise and frustrated rage. 'A riddle, yes. Curse you, mortal!' it bellows. For a moment you think it is going to attack you, but then it subsides. 'You have won your passage with honour, and you are free to go. Before you do, listen to my words:

'If you should find yourself in the Tourney of the Planes, and it comes to pass that you slay the Dai-Oni, invoke the Jizo of Demons thus: "A Sura is here, O Jizo. Come and execute your purpose."'

With that cryptic message, the Tatsu takes to the air and is gone. In its place is a jade talisman, shaped like a dragon. You pick it up and examine it. It is a Talisman of Fortuitous Circumstance. Add 2 to your LUCK. You press on through the wood. Turn to **82**.

53

Standing with your back to the white waters, you heft your heavy sword. But the treacherous slime sends you off balance. Your sword flashes past the monster's head and it grips you in its powerful claws. They rake you for 4 STAMINA points of damage. If you are still alive, the scaly green man flings your body into the frothing white water below the ford as if you were no more than a rag doll. Unfortunately for you the monsters have concealed sharpened stakes just below the surface, upon which you are now impaled. Lose 4 more STAMINA points. If you still live, you painfully drag yourself off the stakes, which have punctured your armour in several places, and are washed up on the far bank. Turn to **395**.

54

You have finally defeated the Dai-Oni and it lies at your feet in the sand of the Arena, breathing its last. The ghostly crowd fades away and the Arena is empty. The Dai-Oni whispers painfully to you, 'You have won, mortal. The laws of the Tourney of the Planes, set by the gods, bind me like fetters of steel. Now I must grant you one request.' What will you ask:

'What is the Secret of Singing Death?'	Turn to **206**
'How do I slay Ikiru, Master of Shadows?'	Turn to **188**
'Help me in my quest to slay Ikiru.'	Turn to **150**

55

Once more the magician anticipates your approach. 'Almost the last trial,' he beams 'You have done well, young Samurai.' The priestess starts to tremble as you near the gaping jaws and the fins of the Sea Dragon, which is covered in serried spikes. The Dragon rears its head as the magician departs once more, and then a gushing torrent of boiling water swamps you both. The screams of the priestess ring in your ears as you lose consciousness and the Sea Dragon swallows you whole.

56

The Samurai rider starts at the sight of you. Then he shouts, 'It is that milksop, the so-called Shogun, Kihei Hasekawa's lackey! Long live the new Shogun, Tsietsin-Sama!' He levels his spear and charges at you. Lord Tsietsin has turned traitor. If you are a master of the bow and wish to fire an arrow, turn to **80**. If not, you will have to receive his charge: turn to **92**.

57

The disembodied heads begin to scream and curse horribly, smashing their skulls into your face and arms. You struggle on, but are soon staggering, punch-drunk and unable to defend yourself. The Rokuro-Kubi are stripping the flesh from your bones even as you collapse. They will dine well tonight.

58

Once again it leaps back to the other end of the bridge. It turns fully visible once more and gives a strange ululating cry. To your horror the skeletal bodies floating in the bloody river stir and come to life. Six of them begin to climb on to the bridge. If you have the skill of Kyujutsu and wish to try to shoot the undead Samurai, turn to **134**. If not, turn to **242**.

59

The charcoal-burners number about ten and they are clustered within a circle of low smoking mounds which are covered by newly cut turf. Grey smoke rises from the mounds that conceal the wood which is slowly being turned into charcoal at great heat. Near by lie several staves ready to be burnt. Will you order them to abase themselves at your feet (turn to **111**), send an arrow winging its way towards the youth, if you have the skill of Kyujutsu (turn to **123**), draw your swords (turn to **135**), or, if you have the skill of Karumijutsu, leap heroically among them (turn to **147**)?

60

You draw your sword, shouting, 'You must help me, or take the consequences!' Her face blanches, full of fear and terror, but then she points at you and a bolt of blue energy flies from her hands to explode in front of you, an incandescent sheet of blue flame that jolts you painfully. Lose 2 STAMINA points. If you still live, when you look again she has gone. If you wish to follow her, turn to **70**. Otherwise you can step through the door and return to the Hub. In this case, return to **8** and choose another option, but not one you have tried already.

61

Halfway across the ford your feet slide out from beneath you as you slip on the treacherous slime and pitch headlong into the frothing white water. Unfortunately for you the Kappa – for that is what the scaly green men are called – have placed sharpened stakes just below the surface. You are impaled and without the protection of your armour there is no hope of ever prising yourself off the painful trap.

62

You thrust your sword deep into one of its black eyes and it rears back, uttering a shrill burbling shriek. It threshes wildly in its death-throes and you have to leap back out of the way. Presently it subsides and falls dead. A search of the cavern reveals an exit at one end, and a heaped pile of 'treasure' –

mostly bones and old useless weapons. However, you do find 15 Gold Pieces, a shiny silver helmet of ornate workmanship, a bottle of greenish-black ichor-like liquid and a magnificently crafted iron war-fan, used in battles to signal troops, inlaid with a pattern of ivory that makes you feel nauseous to look at. Will you:

Pick up the war-fan and open it?	Turn to **182**
Drink some of the liquid?	Turn to **196**
Put on the helmet?	Turn to **210**
Leave them all and go through the exit?	Turn to **222**

63

You hurl the sword at the throne. It flies like an arrow towards its target. As it touches the ring of shadows around the throne, it bursts into light. In a flash of bright whiteness they are all burnt out of existence. The light reveals Ikiru cowering in his robes on the throne, but at the last moment, the Master of Shadows dodges aside and the sword embeds itself in his throne, where it stays, quivering.

Singing Death is now out of your hands. The power it lent you is gone. Lose 4 STAMINA points, 2 SKILL points and 2 LUCK points. Ikiru gets to his feet and whispers, 'You fool.' His voice is like a rustle of leaves. Turn to **260**.

64

You walk forward; the Shikome, giving off an odour like rancid butter, regard you with dull, uninterested eyes. You take them by surprise and leap to the attack. Within seconds you have slain one, but the other begins to howl wildly in fear. In moments the castle is swarming with Samurai and Shikome. You try to escape, but are soon spotted and are buried under a wave of attackers. They take you prisoner, making gibes about the Shogun and his champion as they do so – they plainly know who you are.

You are unceremoniously thrown into a small cell in the palace dungeon. The gaoler, a large beefy man in a stained leather jerkin, says jeeringly, 'You will be taken before the Shogun Tsietsin on the morrow.' Then he slams the massive, iron-studded, oaken door of the cell in your face.

You are alone. They have taken your swords, and it is this rather than the cruel gibes and the indignity of capture that fills you with shame. Lose 1 Honour point for their loss. There is nothing you can do but wait for the morning, so you lie down on the wooden pallet in the corner and go to sleep. Turn to **316**.

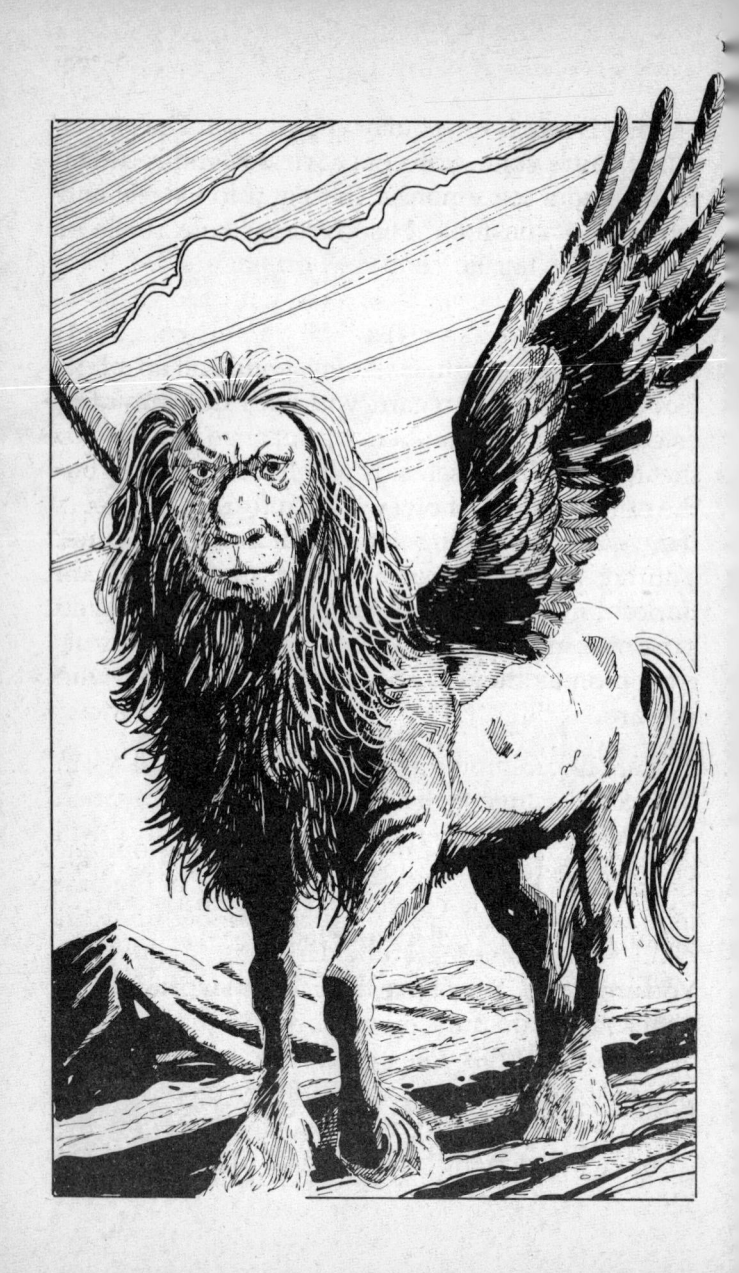

65

Dusk comes and still you have not succeeded in freeing your leg from the chafing trap. A prickling sensation runs up and down your back: you are convinced that the charcoal-burners are watching and waiting. The night is alive with the rustle of leaves and small animals; then you are jolted into vivid awareness by silence. The wind has dropped, but the noises of all the animals have stopped, apart from the padding of a heavy but stealthy beast. You can hear it snuffling along your trail, then a great roar sends a flock of birds screeching into the night. You guess it must be a Shako-Gurubi, a forest panther. You are almost helpless, trapped in the darkness. Will you seize your katana and cut off your own leg below the knee so that you can at least limp free and defend yourself (turn to **119**), or flail the sword blindly and hope that it doesn't attack (turn to **139**)?

66

You step through the door marked 'The Mountain of Ineffable Holiness'. You are standing at the base of a tall mountain peak – easily climbed, but the climb would be long and exhausting. There is no visible means of leaving this place; you have little choice but to go up.

At last, you heave yourself over the lip on to a flattish area at the top of the mountain. You gasp in surprise at the sight that greets you. A strange being of noble stature, radiating an aura of grace and

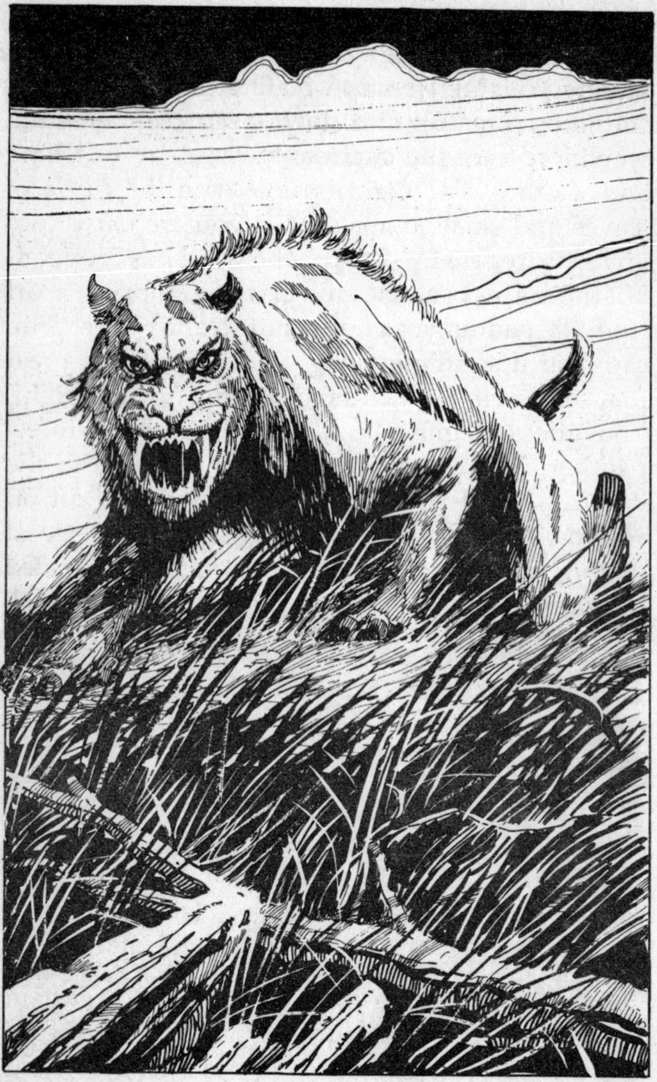

power, looks down at you, its eyes twin orbs of flame. It has a horse's body, with a lion-like head and huge feathered wings. It is a Ki-Rin, a servitor of the gods, a creature of wisdom, a representative and warrior of law and goodness.

It looks you up and down for a moment. If your Honour is 5 or more, turn to **340**. If it is less than 5, turn to **352**.

67

The trident's tines have pierced your armour and broken two of your ribs. Lose 4 STAMINA points. If you are still alive, you decide that discretion is the better part of valour and leave the vicinity of the ford. Turn to **335**.

68

You step through the door marked 'The Elder Plain'. Before you stretches a breathtaking vista. A grassy plain, studded with low hills and copses, stretches away in all directions under a bright blue sky. The air is the freshest and purest you have ever breathed. Near by a strange primitive-looking deer bounds past. Directly behind you, a door hangs in the air, the return route to the Hub.

Then a massive animal appears. It is a huge sabre-toothed tiger. It stares fixedly at you, and breaks into a lope, which soon speeds up into a full-fledged run. What will you do? Take out the Phoenix Ruby, if you have it (turn to **214**), fire an arrow at the tiger, if you have that skill (turn to **224**), blow a horn, if you have one (turn to **234**), or step back through the door (return to **8** and choose again, but not an option you have already tried)?

69

The disembodied heads begin to scream and curse horribly, smashing their skulls into your face and arms. You struggle on, but are soon staggering, punch-drunk and unable to defend yourself. In the confusion, you have staggered back to the well and you fall head over heels sixty feet into cold water below. Turn to **25**.

70

You follow her trail into the wood, but moments later it seems to vanish without trace. You wander aimlessly through the woods, but soon you are completely lost. It is as if the woods shift and change continuously. You are doomed to wander the Enchanted Wood for eternity. Perhaps one day you may stumble across the young woman. Your adventure ends here.

71

The first peasant you meet is a middle-aged woman with her head swathed in a tatty silk scarf. She seems to be plunged into melancholy, but she takes you to her dwelling, a low wooden building with a hole in the side of one of the screens. There is a straw-filled mattress for you to sleep on and hot gruel on the stove. Will you mend the woman's house (turn to **215**), or eat the gruel and settle down to sleep (turn to **203**)?

72

With a powerful scything blow you cut deep into the rider's leg. He gives a shout of pain and topples from the saddle. Before he hits the ground, you have struck his head from his shoulders with one sweep of your katana.

Lord Tsietsin is a traitor, you realize: about ten of his Samurai are running amok in the village, looting and killing the defenceless villagers. Will you leave the village to its fate, deciding your mission is more important (turn to **104**)? Or will you run into the village and attack the nearest Samurai (turn to **116**)? Or will you run into the village and shout out that you are the Shogun's champion and you challenge anyone to an honourable duel (turn to **128**)? Or, if you have the skill of Kyujutsu, will you enter the village and dodge from house to house, picking off the raiders as you go (turn to **140**)?

73

Cautiously you inch your way across the pier of rock which is only a few inches below the surface of the river. The green slime which covers the rock is treacherous underfoot. Two scaly green monsters surge powerfully up from the green depths and climb nimbly on to the pier of rock. They have vicious webbed claws and seem untroubled by the slime underfoot. Will you hurtle yourself off the ford into the frothing white water (turn to **49**), retreat from the ford and run, hoping to find a safer place to cross the river (turn to **105**), or, if you have the skill of Kyujutsu, try to scare them off using a humming-bulb arrow (turn to **21**)?

74

You have finally defeated the Dai-Oni and it lies at your feet in the sand of the Arena, breathing its last. The ghostly crowd fades away and the Arena is empty. The Dai-Oni whispers painfully to you, 'You have won, mortal. The laws of the Tourney of the Planes, set by the gods, bind me like fetters of steel.

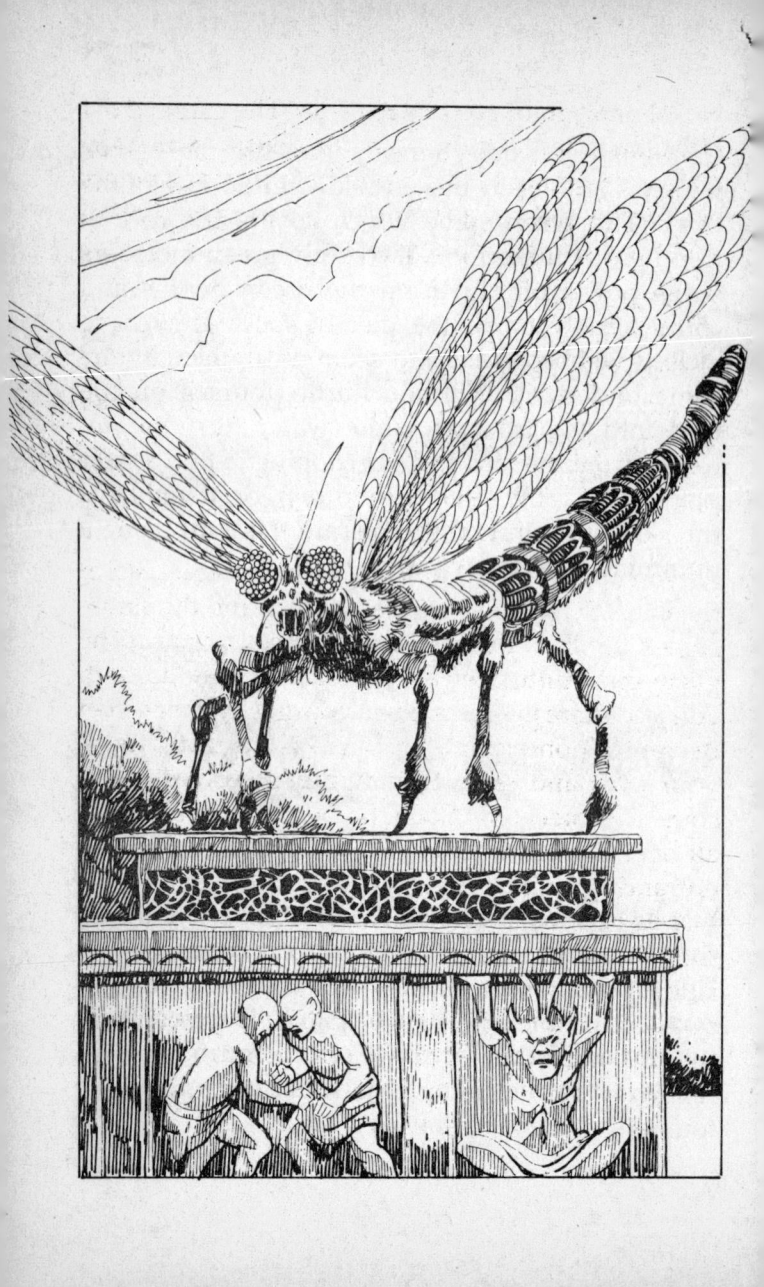

Now I must grant you one request.' The magic of the Dai-Oni fades a little with its defeat. You may restore 1 point of SKILL, 1 point of LUCK or 2 points of STAMINA, if you lost any of these in your battle. What will you ask of the Dai-Oni:

'What is the Secret of
  Singing Death?'   Turn to **206**
'How do I slay Ikiru,
  Master of Shadows?'   Turn to **188**
'Help me in my quest to
  slay Ikiru.'   Turn to **150**

75

As you approach the statue of Hammurabi, Lord of the Flies, the magician appears again and the statue comes to life, flexing its forty-foot wings. The glistening multi-faceted eyes seem to stare through you and there is a buzzing all around. The magician disappears once more and insects begin to attack your eyes and skin. Hammurabi's servants have come to protect him. Soon the swarm is inches thick all over you, but the priestess begins to chant an entrancing lullaby. It is the Song of Swarms. The insects become sleepy and start to fall off you until they litter the ground. The priestess continues her singing and you see that Hammurabi's body is swaying in time with her chant. She is an acolyte of the cult of the Lord of the Flies. She bows down in reverence before Hammurabi and your way to the fountain is open. Turn to **95**.

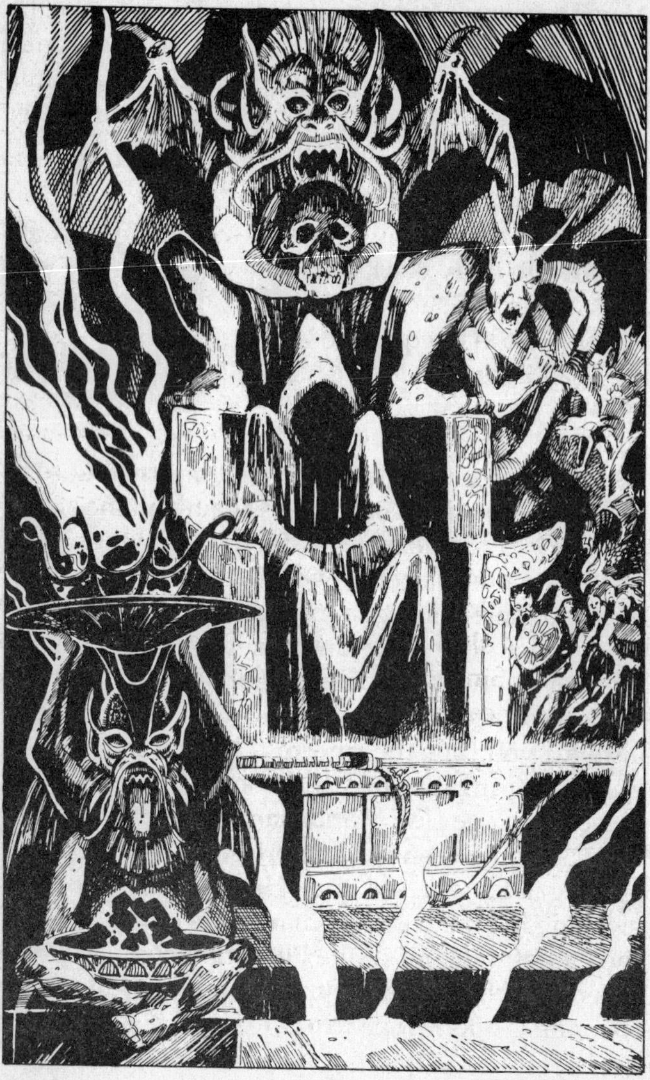

76

The walls of the Arena begin to shimmer, fade and dissolve away. Something else appears in its stead, a black, dark place. You are at the end of a long, pillared hall of black marble. Braziers of glowing coal give off an eerie glow and shadows flicker and weave, chasing one another across the floor. At the end of the hall is a huge pit, from which noxious fumes spiral upward. Beyond the pit is a grotesquely carved throne of dull stone. The workmanship is extraordinary; peaks, pinnacles, gargoyles and strange twisted shapes adorn it. The effect is to wreathe the throne in shadows. You can just make out a cowled figure sitting upon it. It seems to be staring at something in front of the throne. On a stand before the throne rests a magnificent no-dachi, a two-handed sword, in a scabbard of bright filigreed gold. It seems completely out of place in this hall of shadowy gloom and brooding evil. You recognize Singing Death, the Sword of the Samurai, and your heart is uplifted.

Then the cowled head jerks up in surprise. Beneath the cowl there is nothing but blackness. A sibilant whisper hisses forth, a quiet exhalation of breath. 'Who dares to visit Onikaru, the Pit of Demons, and incur the wrath of Ikiru, Master of Shadows?'

If you know the secret of Singing Death, turn to **152**. If you do not, turn to **94**.

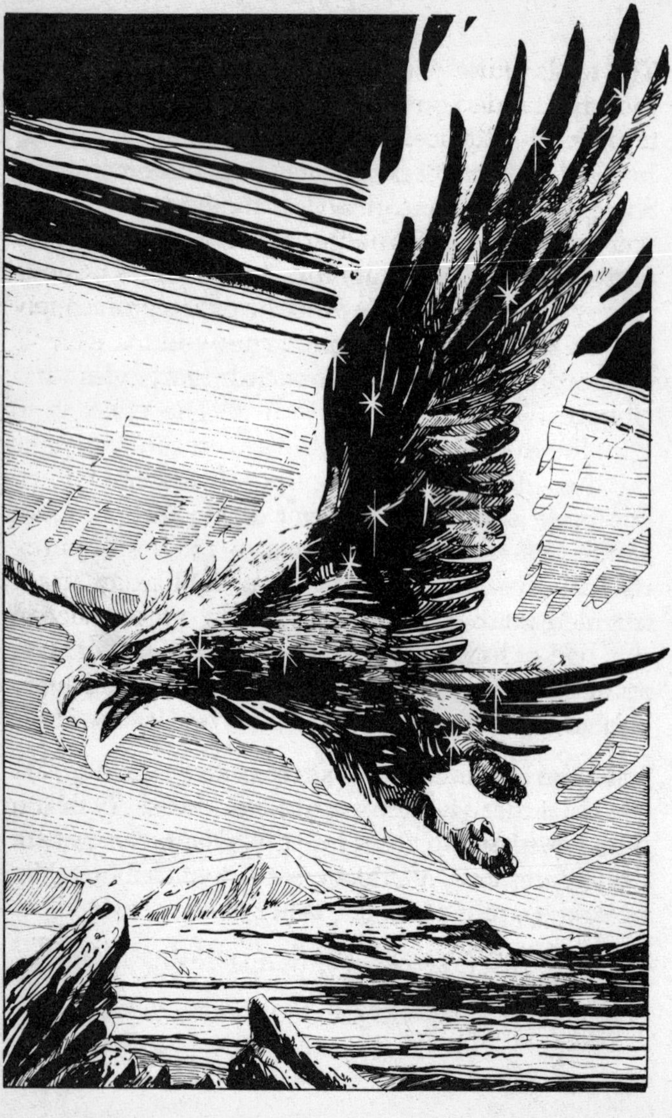

77

You walk quickly past the smoking turf-covered mounds tended by the charcoal-burners and they taunt you with cries that you have deserted the Shogun and are fleeing Hachiman in fear lest the Shogun fall and his favourites be executed. Indeed, you could expect no better, for it has sometimes been your duty to kill traitors and enemies of your master and their families will never forget you. Your conscience is troubled, for you have failed to defend the good name of the Shogun. Subtract 1 from your Honour. Turn to **93**.

78

You step through the door marked 'The Endless Sands of Akhon'. Instantly beads of sweat appear on your forehead as your body is assailed by a terrible heat. Below a yellow sky, in which hangs a sun larger than you have ever seen, stretches mile upon mile of desert – the endless sands of Akhon. Behind you hangs a door, the way back to the Hub.

Suddenly a harsh cry, an ear-splitting shriek, fills the air. A strange bird is arrowing down out of the sky. It is larger than the largest eagle and its eyes are red and glowing. Its feathers are gold and metallic-looking, but the strangest thing of all is that yellow flame seems to play lightly all over it, without consuming it. It is a Phoenix. If you have the Phoenix Ruby, turn to **348**. If not, turn to **360**.

79

It is not long before you are attacked by another giant trap-door spider which launches itself out of its burrow just at the moment when a gangly-legged water spider scuttles up to attack you. You must fight them both.

	SKILL	STAMINA
TRAP-DOOR SPIDER	10	12
WATER SPIDER	8	10

If you win, turn to **87**.

80

The Samurai rider is wearing heavy battle armour. You will have to use armour-piercer arrows against him. You may fire your bow twice before the rider reaches you. Roll two dice for each shot: if the result is less than your SKILL, then the arrow draws blood and your target loses 2 STAMINA points.

Then he closes in, his spear aimed at your throat. Turn to **92**, but remember to deduct any STAMINA loss you inflicted on the Samurai with your arrows.

81

The battle rages on, but when you have struck blows that would have killed any normal man, the silver Samurai falls to his knees and offers his head to your blade, as if acknowledging your mastery. You cannot harm him and so you bid him rise. 'You fought bravely and nobly. I shall bear my sword beside you as you take your next steps in the Enchanted Garden,' he says. Will you now take the path that leads to the priestess and the demon statues (turn to **185**), or that which leads to Hammurabi, the Lord of the Flies (turn to **165**)?

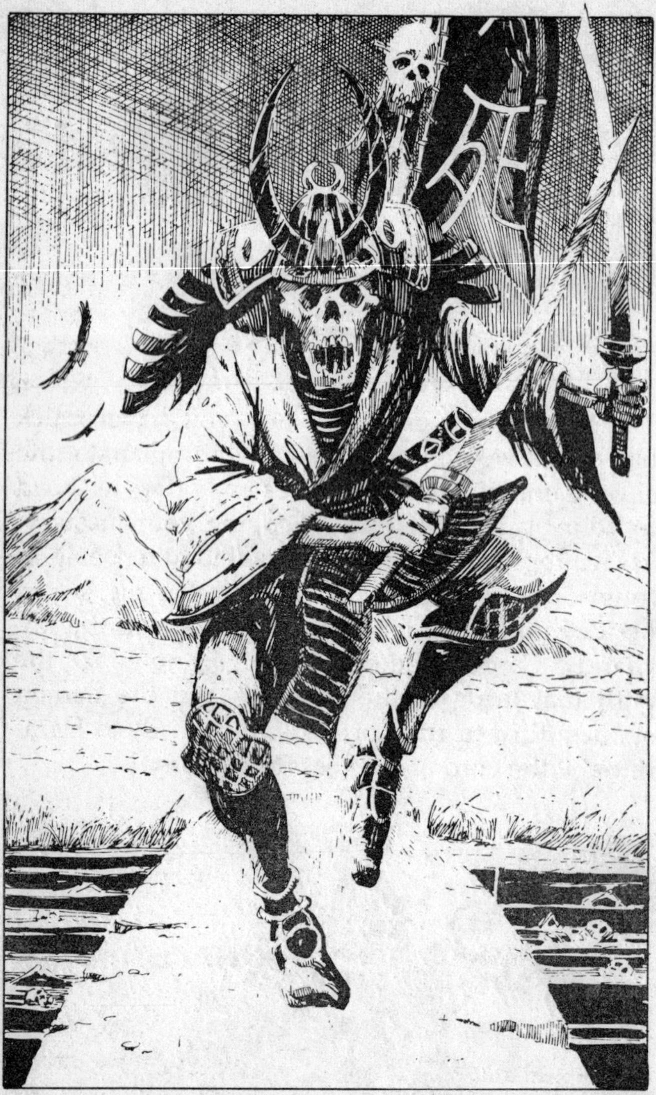

82

Eventually you come out of the Forest of Shadows. In front of you the track becomes a road that runs across an ancient stone bridge, over a river. It is the Hiang-Kiang River, and the bridge is the Hagakure Bridge. Beyond it, on the horizon, rise the Shios'ii Mountains.

As you walk on to the bridge everything around you changes; it is as if you had stepped into another world. All the landmarks are the same – the bridge, the mountains and so on – but the sky is darker now. The river to either side of the bridge is red as blood and skeletal bodies, skulls, bones and limbs float on its surface.

Before you stands a hideous apparition. It is a Samurai warrior, but one who has been long dead. A grinning skull rests inside the helmet and each skeletal hand clutches a sword. The flag attached to its back, adorned with skulls, reads 'Evil Death'. The undead warrior leaps into the air and comes down before you. You must fight it.

UNDEAD SAMURAI   SKILL 9   STAMINA 11

If you reduce its STAMINA to 5 or less, turn to **32**.

83

Hoping to give battle before the green men can drag your armour into the gloomy depths, you race across the pier of rock, which is only inches below the surface of the river. Unfortunately the green slime that covers the pier is extremely slippery. *Test your Luck*, but add 1 to the dice score because you are trying to dash heedlessly across the ford. If you are Lucky, turn to **97**. If you are Unlucky, turn to **61**.

84

You cross the courtyard and walk up to the Shikome. They reek of rancid butter and eye you dully. 'I have an important message for Lord Tsietsin,' you say, trying to sound authoritative. One of them grunts and growls, 'Password.' Realizing you don't know it, you hesitate. 'Well?' growls the Shikome, readying his spear. If you have the skill of Iaijutsu, turn to **252**. If not, turn to **268**.

85

You have shattered the heads of many of the elders, but several more are now crowding in around you. You must flee. *Test your Luck*. If you are Lucky, turn to **45**. If you are Unlucky, turn to **57**.

86

You put the horn to your lips and blow an ear-shattering blast, but all the woman does is clap her hands over her ears and shriek in pain before running away into the forest. If you wish to follow her, turn to **70**. Otherwise you can step through the door and return to the Hub. In this case, return to **8** and choose another option, but not one you have tried already.

87

There are no more spiders to impede your progress and you forge on. The rain lifts a little and the water-level drops to reveal a long dyke leading north out of the Spider Fens. The dyke takes you as far as the foothills of the Shios'ii mountains, where you use goat-tracks to speed your journey. At last you are climbing one of the taller peaks. Turn to **8**.

88

You catch the guard's sword-arm and twist, sending him crashing into the wall where he slumps unconscious. You may take his sword, restoring your SKILL to normal, but he does not have a wakizashi or shortsword. If you have the skill of Ni-to-Kenjutsu, you cannot use it until you have another shortsword. Nor may you use Kyujutsu until you get another bow.

The corridor ends at a stairwell. The steps go up and down. Will you ascend the stairs (turn to **108**) or descend them (turn to **122**)?

89

Stressing the wise ways of the Shogun, you tell them of your mission. Unfortunately these peasants are not loyal to your lord, and they hope he never regains Singing Death. You can only watch as they bring a cartload of glowing charcoal from one of the ovens and empty it all over you. It is a painful but quick death.

90

The Dai-Oni casts a spell with its other hand, sending a burst of electrical energy through its iron club. Lose an extra 2 STAMINA points. If you still live, return to **292** and fight on.

91

Inside the cave, a beautiful woman lies on a ledge of stone. Her eyes sparkle malevolently as she invites you to dine with her on the heart of a human baby. You reply that you are an honourable Samurai and will not come near her. The beautiful woman changes into a wizened and demonic hag before your very eyes. She is a Nushi, a monster appearing as a beautiful woman who can command all the beasts around her den to do her will. 'Then you must fight my pets, Samurai,' she says. She calls flutingly, and the cave entrance is blocked by three giant spiders, a trap-door spider which leaps almost on top of you, a powerful earth spider and a gangly legged water spider. Maybe you could have defeated two of them, but not three such monsters together. Your adventure ends here.

92

The spear-head hurtles towards you. Roll two dice: if the result is less than or equal to your SKILL, you have successfully parried the thrust. If not, it gashes your shoulder and you lose 3 STAMINA points.

In any case, the Samurai wheels his horse round and stabs down as you try to cut him from the saddle.

SAMURAI WARRIOR   SKILL 8   STAMINA 9

If you win, turn to **72**.

93

The taunts of the charcoal-burners sail down the breeze as you turn a bend in the road that skirts the wood where they cut the staves to be turned into charcoal. The cracking of dry twigs alerts you as four of the peasants, brandishing staves, run out in an attempted ambush. The other charcoal-burners are not far behind, having used a trail through the wood as a short cut. You put your back to a tree, so that no more than two can attack at a time. You must give battle.

	SKILL	STAMINA
First CHARCOAL-BURNER	6	10
Second CHARCOAL-BURNER	7	9

If you kill the first of your attackers without being hurt, turn to 347. If you have been wounded by the time you have killed one of them, turn to 365.

94

You advance resolutely down the hall, determined to slay Ikiru. The figure on the throne gives a ghostly laugh, a faint spine-tingling titter of madness. Then it gestures. To your horror, a shadowy form floats up out of the pit and takes shape before you. It is vaguely man-like, but with a horned head and massive taloned claws. It is a Shadow Demon, only semi-corporeal, a creature from the nether regions, and you must fight it.

SHADOW DEMON SKILL 9 STAMINA 10

Each time you hit it, roll one die. If the result is even, it loses 2 STAMINA points. If the result is odd, your blow does not connect fully, passes through some of its insubstantial flesh and it loses only 1 point of STAMINA. If you defeat it, turn to **260**.

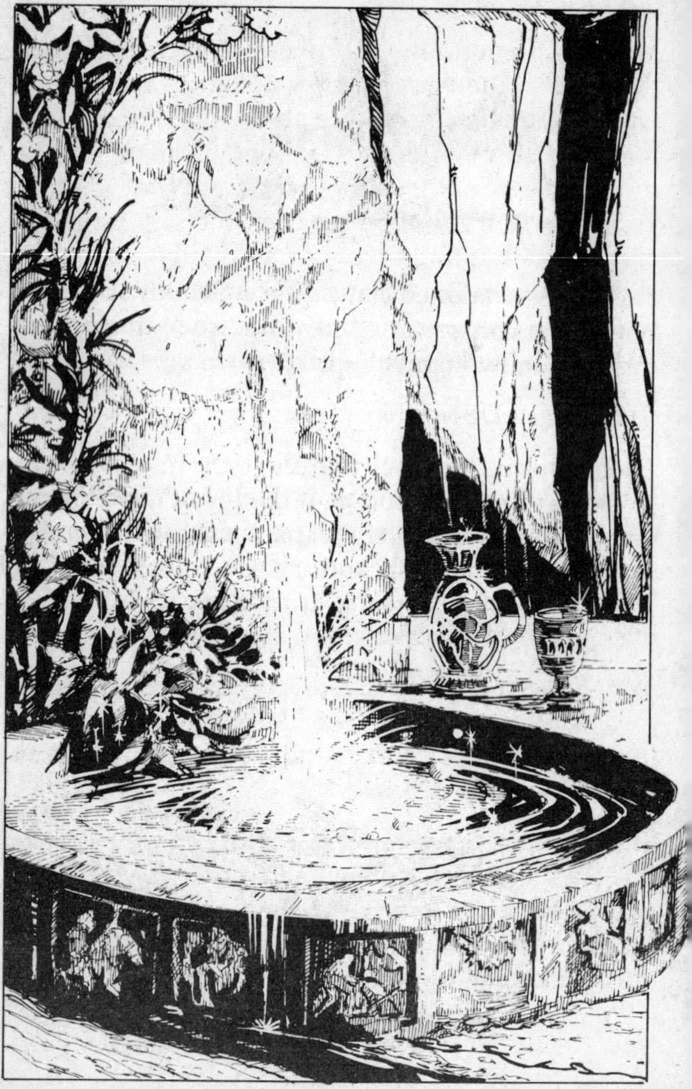

95

You walk beyond the shimmering magnificence of the Lord of the Flies to the fountain. A cascade of water pours forth from the centre of a large white rock into the marble-rimmed pool. Climbing plants mirror the arc of the falling water and they glisten, kept forever wet by the spray thrown up from the cascade. Set upon one of the marble blocks at the side of the pool is a silver ewer and a chalice. The waters are clear and cool. If you wish to drink from them, turn to **161**. If you decide to fill the ewer, turn to **243**.

96

Her wits seem addled in some way. Perhaps Waters of Knowledge may help to clear them. You offer the bottle to her. Without thought, she listlessly takes the bottle, and gulps it down. She freezes instantly, her eyes suddenly filling with bright intelligence.

'I am Eleanor the Enchantress. It was Ikiru who sent me insane with a spell!' She looks at you gratefully. 'And I know of you and your quest. I shall be at your side in the Place of Battle.'

She bows and leaves the glade. Note on your *Adventure Sheet* that Eleanor the Enchantress is your ally. Now you must return to the Hub, by passing through the door. Return to **8** and choose another option, but not one you have already tried.

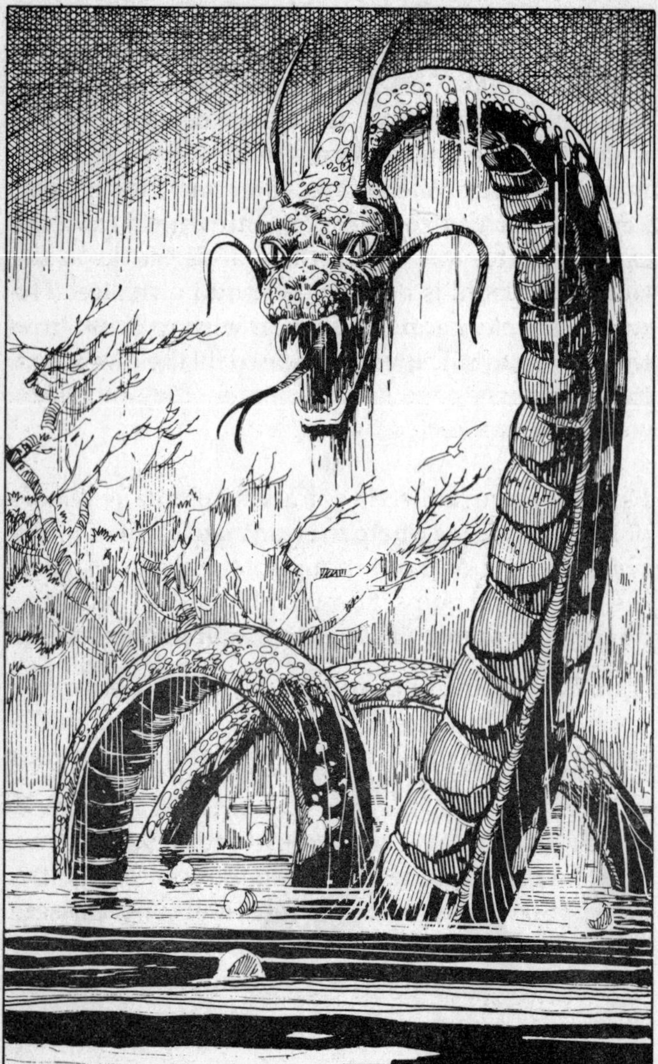

97

Halfway across the ford your feet slide out from beneath you as you slip on the treacherous slime. You are about to pitch headlong into the frothing white water below the ford when your foot catches against a large water-snail and you regain your balance enough to teeter to the other bank. You are too late to stop the scaly green monsters throwing your armour into the river, and then they turn to give battle. You take on the first three. They have vicious webbed claws which will do 3 STAMINA points of damage to you every time they hit, since you are not protected by armour.

	SKILL	STAMINA
First KAPPA	8	14
Second KAPPA	8	12
Third KAPPA	7	13

If you reduce one of the Kappa to 4 STAMINA points or less, turn to **31**.

98

You find yourself standing on a low hummock of solid earth. Around you lies a great swamp. It bubbles and heaves, a morass of stinking mud and thick liquid. Twisted trees and plants struggle up out of the mess. A door hangs behind you in space, the route back to the Hub.

Suddenly a tremendous serpent, with eyes glittering like black diamonds, bursts out of the mire and rears up before you, ready to whip its head down and bite you in two. If you wish to fight the serpent, turn to **246**. If you would rather try to use an item against it, turn to **258**.

99

You are completely without Honour. As you cast your mind back over your actions since you began your quest for Singing Death, you realize that you acted dishonourably at almost every turn. Without Honour you are nothing, your life is worthless. There is only one honourable action left to you. You must commit seppuku, take your own life. You summon up the courage necessary to fall upon your katana, and drive yourself forward on to the blade until you die. At least in this last detail, the manner of your parting from the world, you have acted according to the code of the Samurai.

100

You walk across the courtyard towards the palace, strutting like a newly appointed general. The Shikome, who reek like rancid butter, eye you dully. As you walk up to them, looking past them as if they were not there, you flash the seal of the Shogun at them, hoping they will not recognize it. Your bold and arrogant manner fools the Shikome completely and they salute smartly as you stride past them into the palace! Turn to **158**.

101

The impudent youth suggests that they sew up your mouth, ears and nose before they kill you, so that your spirit cannot escape your body to haunt them, but the mention of spirits has scared the others into letting you go. The youth sees your baleful glare and leaves while you are being set free. His father, a crook-legged old fellow, creaks painfully to his knees and humbly begs your pardon for the insulting behaviour of his son. The others follow suit as he offers to show you a safe village near by, where you may stay the night. Will you make them swear an oath of allegiance before going on (turn to **163**), or command the old man to show you to the sanctuary of the village (turn to **179**)?

102

The Dai-Oni laughs and steps back. It mutters arcane words and casts a Spell of Misfortune on you. Lose 1 LUCK point. Return to **292** and fight on.

103

All goes still for a moment as you lie prone on the ledge, then there is a dull rumbling from the earth and the ground starts to shake once more. The tremor is strong and there is a great cracking noise in the wall of slate. The ceiling of the cave crashes down with an enormous report and slivers of grey rock fly everywhere. If you had taken refuge in the cave mouth, you would have been flattened. Turn to **273**.

104

You turn around and leave, heading back to the main road. The cries of the defenceless villagers echo across the uncaring countryside. Lose 1 Honour point for your callous action. Turn to **24**.

105

There is no pursuit as you hastily leave the ford behind you. You have lost your armour, and without its protection you will lose 3 STAMINA points instead of 2 every time you are hit in battle. The Shogun's champion is supposed to acquit himself more nobly than this. Without your armour you stand much less chance of succeeding in your quest, and by deserting it you have dishonoured the Shogun, your lord, for it was he who gave it to you. Subtract 2 from your Honour and turn to **263**.

106

You come out of the valley to be faced by a large and forbidding forest, stretching away for miles to either side. The road disappears into its depths like a stone into water. You recognize it as the Forest of Shadows, and you must go through it. Moichi smiles wanly at you and says, 'I have heard only evil about the Forest since the theft of Singing Death, my lord. Must we . . .?' You nod your head: 'Yes, we must, Moichi.' You stride forward. Turn to **124**.

107

The map shows that the path leading to the scarlet pagoda is the westerly path which runs along a dyke at the edge of a mist-covered lake. If you would like to try to follow the route all the way to the scarlet pagoda, turn to **317**. If not, turn to **17** and choose again.

108

You emerge into a small storeroom. A doorway leads out into the castle courtyard. Another leads into the palace itself. Will you go into the palace in search of Tsietsin (turn to **158**), or don the armour of the guard you have just killed and try to bluff your way out through the castle gates (turn to **168**)?

109

Suddenly a stream of shadowy blackness passes from Ikiru's sword and begins to course across your body like a mesh of interwoven cords. Wherever it touches you it burns agonizingly. You stagger back, howling in pain, as the web of blackness begins to constrict, crushing the life out of you.

When you are dead, your spirit is taken into the Pit of Demons, where you will become a servant of Ikiru, to be called upon whenever he should wish to do so.

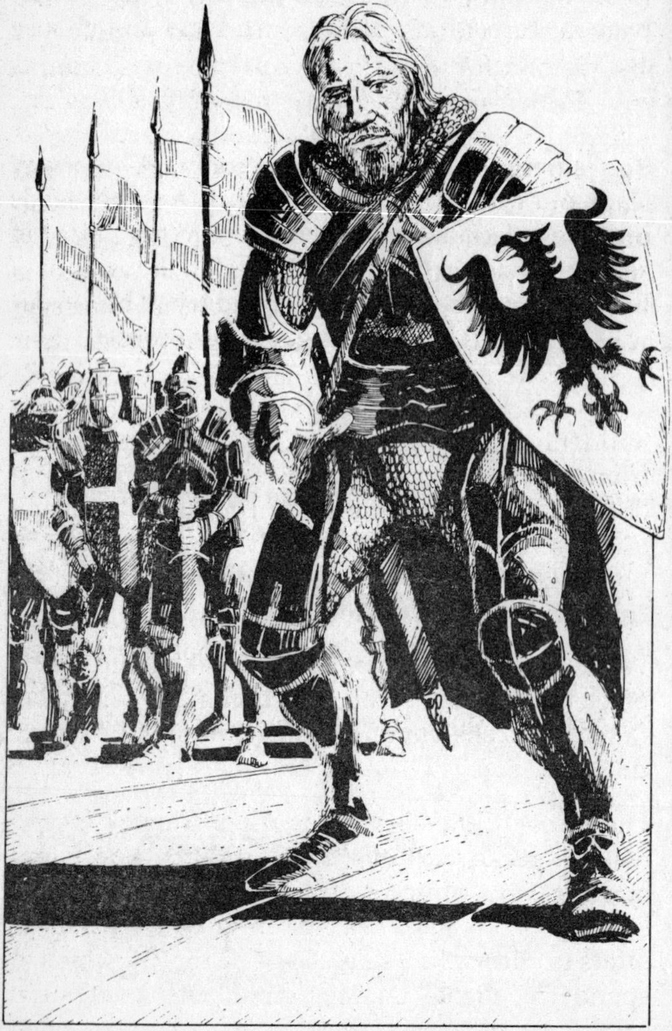

110

You step through the door marked 'The Eternal Tower'. Everything changes. You are standing at the top of a fortified tower; battlements surround you. The terrain around you is constantly changing, sometimes wood, sometimes plains; blue sky, red sky, and so on – as if the Tower were shifting from plane to plane and world to world. In front of you stands a massive warrior, his face bearded and mature, a veteran of many battles. His armour is strange and outlandish to you: it covers him from head to foot. Behind him stand eight others, their faces visored and hidden. Their armour is gold, with a white surcoat covered in blue circles.

The man speaks: 'Welcome to the Eternal Tower, contestant. We are the Knights of the Golden Company, and if you wish us to aid you in the Tourney of the Planes, you must answer me this. Do you return to us the war-fan of our king?'

If you have a war-fan, with a symbol of nine gold arrows, a blue circle and a white background, turn to **186**. If you do not, turn to **200**.

111

The eldest of the charcoal-burners, a crook-legged fellow, creaks painfully to his arthritic knees and humbly begs your pardon for the insulting behaviour of his son. The others follow suit as he offers to show you a safe village near by in which to spend the night. Looking up to see your stern expression he begs you to take his son as a slave that you may teach him humility, but he beseeches you not to kill him. Will you make them swear an oath of allegiance before going on (turn to **163**), or command the old man to show you to the sanctuary of the village (turn to **179**)?

112

You follow the thin woodland trail that winds and bends through the clustered boles of the Forest of Shadows. The trees are so closely packed that only a fraction of the sun's rays filter down, in shafts of dusky light filled with motes of dust that float slowly in the air. It is dim and murky, and the sounds of forest life intrude faintly on the edge of your consciousness as you walk on, as if in a waking dream.

Suddenly you stumble out into a broad clearing, your eyes filled with light. You shake your head to clear it, when a sound in the air causes you to look up. A great dragon is floating down towards you. It has a long sinuous body, like a massive serpent, but with four clawed legs. Its head is horned with great, glaring, amber eyes. It has no wings, but seems to be walking on air. It is a Tatsu, a wingless dragon that can walk on sky, sea and land. It settles before you, hovering a few feet off the ground. Its amber eyes regard you placidly, then it speaks in a rich, deep voice, resonant with knowledge and power:

'Welcome to the heart of the forest, mortal. I am the guardian – and there are certain celestial laws that bind me.' It seems to smile at you, if dragons can be said to smile at all! 'You must answer two riddles I shall put to you. If you answer them correctly, you may pass through the forest. If not, well . . . then I shall eat you. And you cannot run. No one can pass through this forest safely without first dealing with me.' Then it laughs as if its last few words were obvious. Turn to **2**.

113

The silence around you is haunting; the mist kills even the sound of the water lapping at the great columns of stone. Leaping from one to another, you have just gone out of sight of the dyke when the water-level seems to rise all around the nearby pillars of basalt. Suddenly a beast of unimaginably huge dimensions looms out of the lake, causing a tidal wave which sweeps you into the water. The Kraken has risen and its huge tentacles, each as thick as your chest, thrust you whole into its gaping beak. Only giants dare risk the giant's causeway and even they will bring a man or two to appease the Kraken's hunger.

114

You take out the helmet. This woman's wits seemed addled in some way; perhaps the helmet may help to cure her. You offer it to her but her eyes widen in fear. 'No!' she breathes in horror, before fleeing into the woods. If you wish to follow her, turn to **70**. Otherwise you can step through the door and return to the Hub. In this case, return to **8** and choose another option, but not one you have tried already.

115

You have shattered the heads of many of the elders, but scores more are now crowding around you. You must flee. *Test your Luck*. If you are Lucky, turn to **69**. If you are Unlucky, turn to **57**.

116

You dash into the village. People are running about in fear, chased by Tsietsin's Samurai, and some buildings are burning ferociously. Near by, a Samurai in magnificent green and blue lacquered armour is looting the body of an old man he has just slain. The sight of this rebel dishonouring himself and the name of all Samurai in such a manner fills you with disgust. You stride forward and cut him down with one blow, your razor-sharp sword almost slicing him in two. He screams once. Several of the traitor Samurai turn at his shout and three of them spring towards you. One of them recognizes you and says, 'The Shogun's – sorry, the *ex*-Shogun's champion. Kill the mangy, flea-ridden goat!' They come at you in a rush, wildly brandishing their swords. You must fight them all at once. If you have the skill of Karumijutsu, you may subtract 1 from all their Attack Rolls for this combat only, as you jump and leap over them, trying to dodge their blows.

	SKILL	STAMINA
First SAMURAI	6	7
Second SAMURAI	8	8
Third SAMURAI	7	6

If you kill all three of them, turn to **154**.

117

You try to bring your sword down to the green water in a slashing motion in order to slice through the net, but the monster is too quick for you. It flings the net around your shoulders and pulls you from your precarious perch on the slime-covered rock. Your sword does you no good as you are dragged below the surface, surrounded by the scaly green monsters. There is nothing you can do. You have fallen into the hands of the Kappa, from which there is no escape.

118

The Dai-Oni howls in joy and then casts a Spell of Confusion on you. Lose 1 SKILL point. Return to **292** and fight on.

119

With a great cry you hack off your own leg at the second cut, reel from the trap and collapse almost unconscious. Through a mist of pain you hear the beast eating your severed foot, while you tie a strip of leather in a tourniquet to stop the spurting blood. Lose 7 STAMINA points. If you survive, the rest of the night passes in horror, as you try to remain conscious lest the beast attack. In the dawn light you see your mistake: it was not a forest panther but a hyena, which mimics the roar of the big cat. You have crippled yourself for nothing and you will have to turn back in disgrace, for your adventuring days are over.

120

The sound of many drumming hoofs comes to you from ahead. You stop and are about to run up the hillside, when a patrol of twenty or more of Lord Tsietsin's men appears ahead. At the sight of you a shout goes up and they charge forward. You cannot escape and a battle ensues. You fight mightily, slaying several, but there are too many of them and you are overwhelmed. To your horror, they slay Moichi out of hand, calling him a traitor – but you knew him to be the only one among them who was truly loyal. Soon you are securely bound and strapped over a horse's back. 'Lord Tsietsin will be pleased with this little catch,' one of them quips.

They take you to the castle you passed on the road. You are led into the courtyard, where many of Lord Tsietsin's Samurai retainers gather around to laugh and mock you. You are unceremoniously thrown into a small cell in the palace dungeon. The gaoler, a large beefy man in a stained leather jerkin, says jeeringly, 'You will be taken before the Shogun Tsietsin on the morrow.' Then he slams the massive, iron-studded, oaken door of the cell in your face.

You are alone. They have taken your swords, and it is this rather than the cruel gibes and the indignity of capture that fills you with shame. Lose 1 Honour point for their loss. There is nothing you can do but wait for the morning, so you lie down on the wooden pallet in the corner and go to sleep. Turn to **316**.

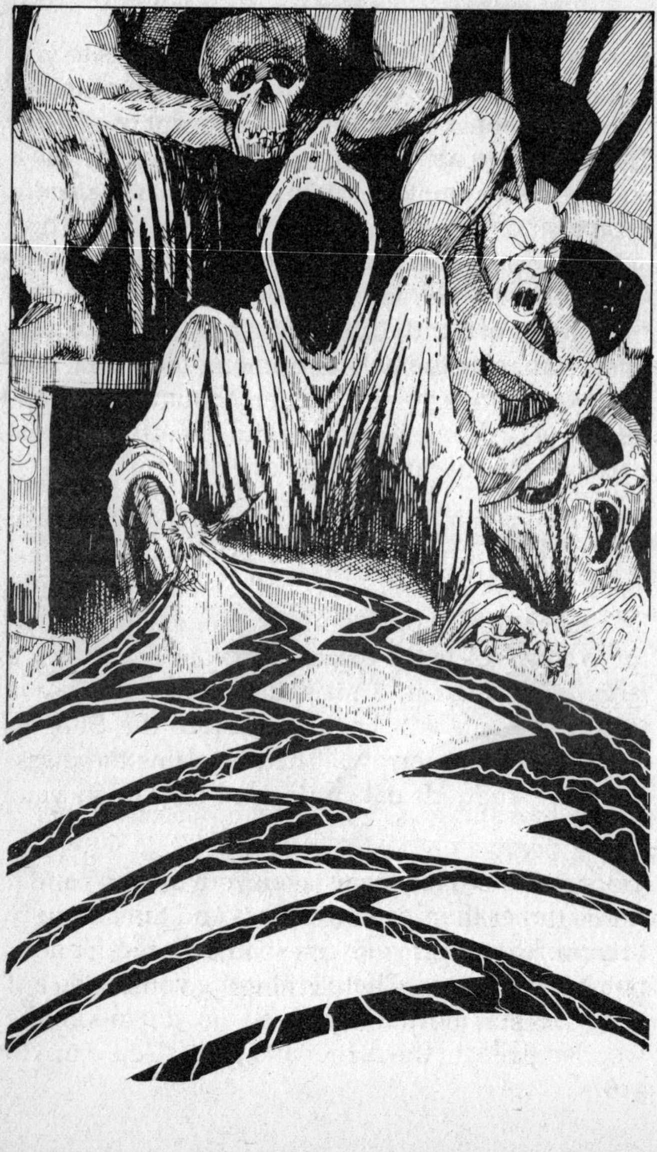

121

You are in front of the throne. Ikiru rises up like a shade; you stare into the cowl, to see only shadowy nothingness, the face of evil. Ikiru points at you and bolts of dark energy leap from his fingers towards you. If your Honour is 6 or more, turn to **189**. If it is 5 or less, turn to **131**.

122

At the bottom of the stairs, a damp, rough-cut tunnel runs ahead into darkness. *Test your Luck*. If you are Lucky, turn to **16**. If you are Unlucky, turn to **38**.

123

In the time it takes a woodpecker to tap the bole of a tree twice, you have sent an arrow winging its way towards the youth. He has no time to dodge. Roll two dice. If the score is less than your SKILL, your aim was true (turn to **207**). If you roll equal to or greater than your SKILL, turn to **351**.

124

As you enter the forest, you feel suddenly alone. Looking back, you cannot see Moichi anywhere. Retracing your steps, you see him running back towards the valley. Obviously his fear of the forest overcame his 'loyalty' to you. Cursing him for a useless coward, among other things, you head back into the forest. Turn to **112**.

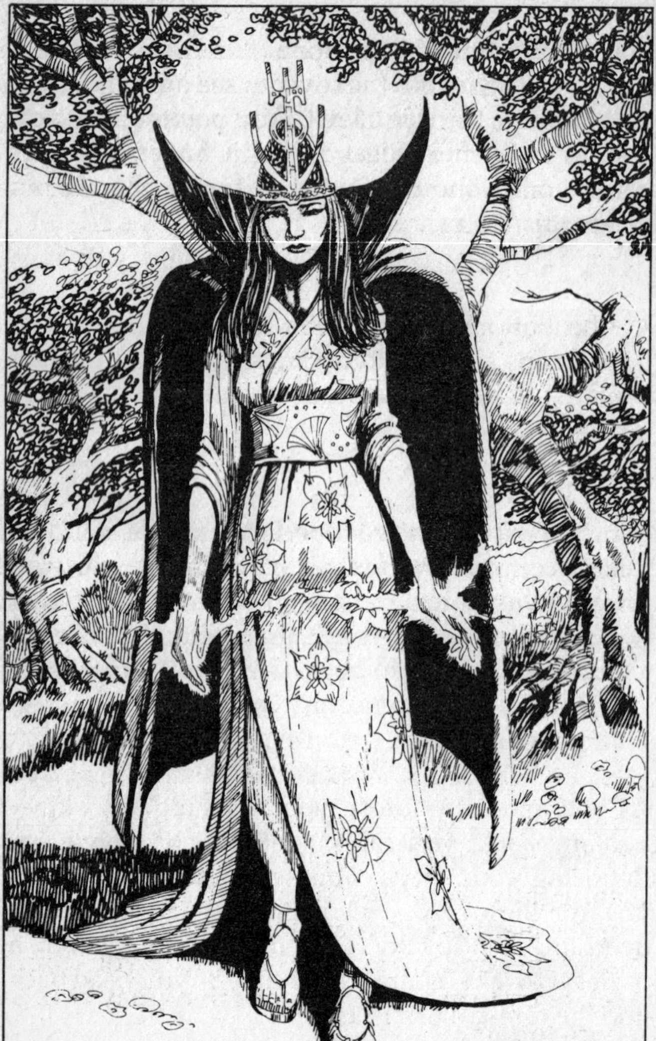

125

The dyke runs for mile upon mile, the product of an ancient civilization that lived in the delta before the eternal mist descended. After a while a winding path leads off into the marsh. If you wish to turn aside on to the path, turn to **339**. If you continue along the dyke, turn to **387**.

126

You open the door marked 'The Enchanted Wood' and step through. You find yourself in a wooded glade. It is strangely quiet, as if no woodland creatures frolicked in this wood. The air is heavy with sorcery – you can almost smell it. You know that if you were to travel in this wood you would become lost in moments, perhaps for ever. Behind you hangs the door to the Hub and you resolve to leave it in sight. Just then, a young woman dressed in rich robes of green steps into the clearing. Her beauty is astounding, but her eyes seem empty and listless. She stares at you vacantly. Oddest of all, a nimbus of crackling blue energy plays about her hands. You ask her who she is and if she will aid you against the Dai-Oni.

'Who am I? I no longer know. As for my aid, that is not lightly won,' she says, her brows knitted in puzzlement as if it is hard for her to speak. Will you attack her and try to force her to help you (turn to **60**), or try to use some item you think may be of use (turn to **48**)?

127

As you run to the ford's edge, three scaly green figures lumber ponderously out of the river and climb the bank at the spot where the other pieces of your armour now lie. They are larger than men, with curiously flat-topped heads, and they move as if balancing an invisible weight on top of them. As you pause, two more break the surface near by. Will you run away, hoping to find a safer place to cross the river (turn to **105**), move slowly across the pier of rock (turn to **73**), or race across to where the scaly monsters are picking up your armour (turn to **83**)?

128

You run into the village and then shout the challenge at the top of your voice. Many of the Samurai turn and stare as you tell them who you are. One of them steps forward and says, 'We no longer owe allegiance to Kihei Hasekawa, and follow the new Shogun, Tsietsin, but we are still Samurai. Come then, let us duel.' He steps forward, drawing his sword. He stands before you, sword raised over his head, its tip pointed at your throat. You must fight three of these Samurai, but they come at you one at a time, in an honourable (but biased) fashion.

	SKILL	STAMINA
First SAMURAI	7	9
Second SAMURAI	9	8
Third SAMURAI	7	9

If you kill all three of them, turn to **190**.

129

Desperate measures are called for if you are to avoid death at the hands of the scaly green monsters. Will you try a trick suggested by the element brimstone (turn to **231**), has the thought of their strange flat-topped heads entered your mind (turn to **255**), or will you perhaps pretend to be about to cast a spell on them (turn to **277**)?

130

This woman's wits seem addled in some way, but there doesn't seem to be anything you can do. If you wish to try to force her to help you, turn to **60**. Otherwise you can return to the Hub by stepping through the door behind you. If you do this, return to **8** and choose again, but not an option you have already tried.

131

The bolts slam into you, simultaneously cursing, charring and crippling you. Lose 1 SKILL, 1 LUCK and 4 STAMINA points. If you are still alive, you reel back and Ikiru hisses with joy. But then you regain your senses and leap toward him wielding Singing Death. Turn to **199**.

132

A voice shouts ahead, 'Hida, is that you?' When you do not reply, there is a muffled curse and the sound of someone running. A guard bursts into the torchlight and gasps in astonishment at the sight of you. 'Escaped? How . . .?' But his sentence is unfinished as you leap to the attack.

GUARD   SKILL 7   STAMINA 9

If you win, turn to **142**.

133

The clacking continues and then suddenly the headman's head lifts cleanly off his shoulders and floats into the air, followed by the heads of everyone else in the village. They are Rokuro-Kubi, you realize in horror, undead whose heads detach from their bodies at night in order to hunt. The flying heads dart at you, jaws snapping viciously. You must fight them as if they were a many-headed monster.

ROKURO-KUBI   SKILL 11   STAMINA 17

If you win, turn to **115**.

134

If you have an arrow with white eagle feathers, crafted by Tsunewara, and wish to fire it, turn to **192**. Otherwise, you draw and loose an ordinary arrow (turn to **164**).

135

One of the charcoal-burners pulls the moist turf from the nearest charcoal oven, and billowing smoke and flame belch forth. Some of them seize staves with which to attack you, others edge nervously back into the woods behind the mounds. *Test your Luck.* If you are Lucky, turn to **293**. If you are Unlucky, turn to **307**.

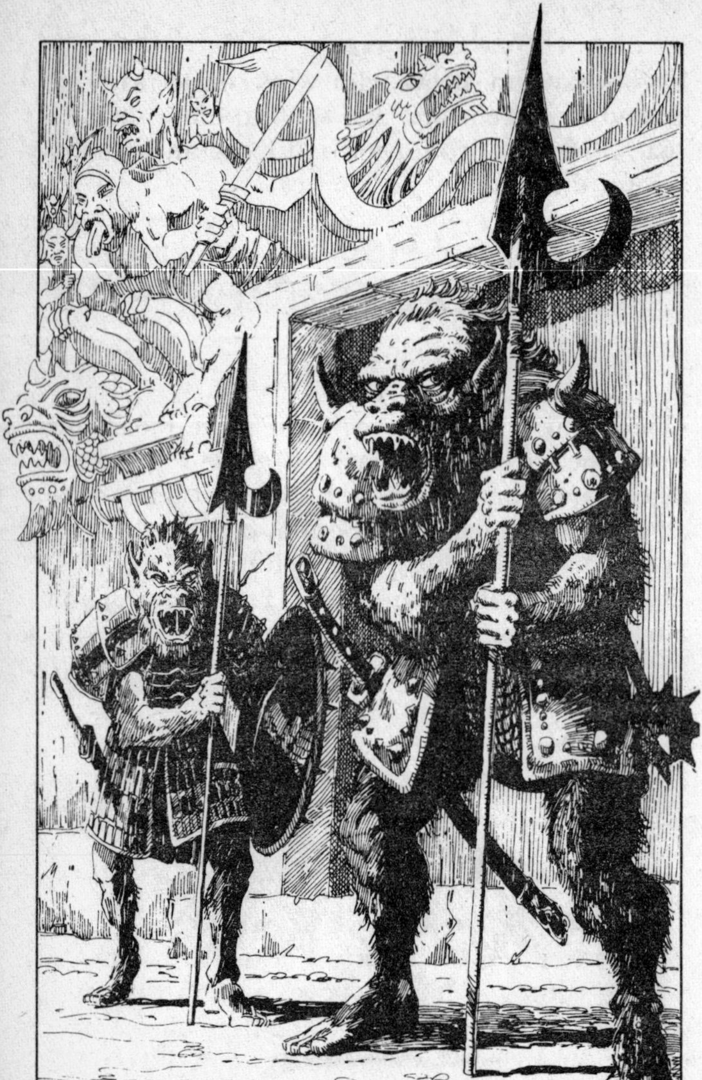

136

You look around. Barracks, stables and so on line the walls. Across the castle courtyard is a square stone keep, with pagoda-like roofs and carved gables, the palace of Lord Tsietsin. But it is the two palace guards flanking the doors that really draw your attention. They are Shikome, vile humanoid beings, but hairy as apes, and with claws, fangs and horrible snouted faces. They are dressed in dirty and tattered imitations of Samurai armour, although their weapons seem in excellent condition. The presence of Shikome can only mean that Tsietsin is in league with Ikiru, Master of Shadows. Tsietsin will be in the palace, and it seems even more important than before to slay him.

Will you disguise yourself in the armour of the guard you have just knocked out, and, with Moichi, approach them, saying you have a message for Lord Tsietsin (turn to **148**), pretend that you are Moichi's prisoner and that he is taking you to see Tsietsin (turn to **160**), or, if you have the skill of Kyujutsu, try to pick off the guards as quickly and as silently as possible (turn to **170**)?

137

A man wearing the ceremonial robes of a court magician steps out from behind a rose hedge and, beaming cordially, bids you welcome to the Enchanted Garden. 'Only by drinking from the spring may you find your way back to the land of Hachiman,' he says. 'You must keep to the paths at all

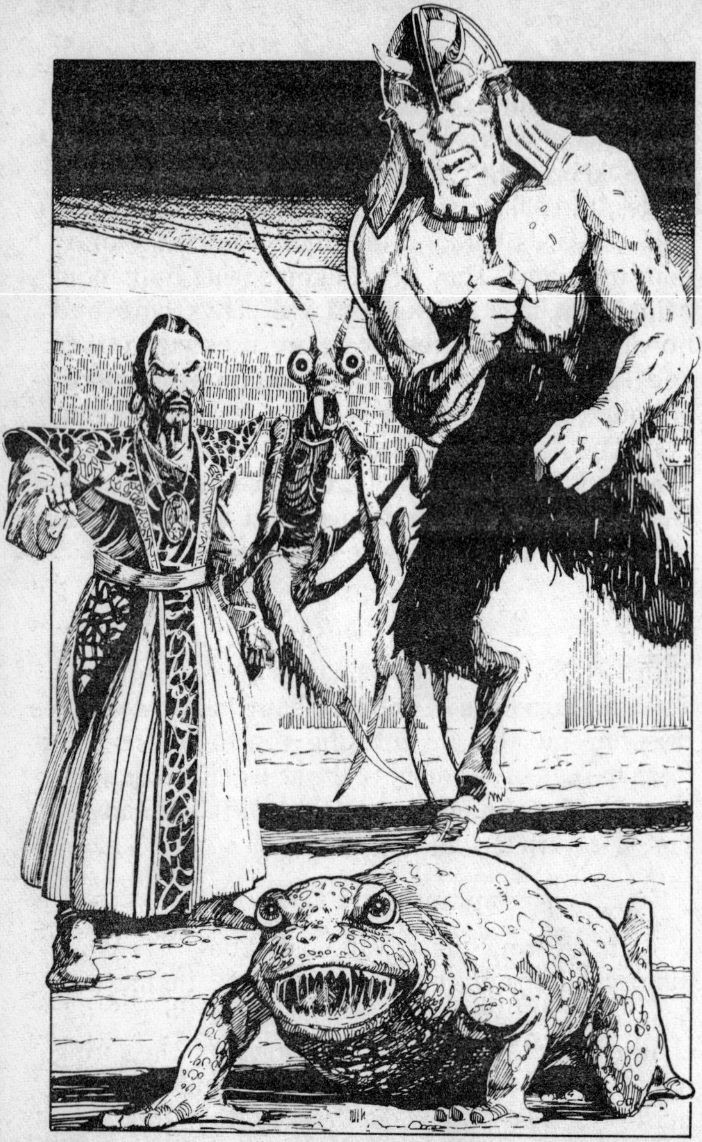

times. This is a place of peril, but if you triumph the reward is high indeed.' With that he disappears in a theatrical puff of smoke. The paths to the fountain all lead past the statues. Will you take the path that leads to the silver Samurai (turn to 379) or to the priestess and the demon (turn to 349)?

138

You have decided you are ready to face the Dai-Oni and his allies, so you open the door marked 'The Place of Battle' and step through. You find yourself in a huge arena, but all the tiered seats are empty – it appears they have been that way for millennia. But as you appear, ghostly figures seem to materialize in the seats, men and women of a bygone age, talking, gesticulating, laying bets on the outcome of the battle, as if they had been waiting for this moment for aeons, even in death.

As you stand on the sandy arena floor, those allies you had noted on your *Adventure Sheet* appear behind you, each saying, or silently imparting, a message of reassurance and support. If you have not managed to win any allies, then you stand alone.

Before you stands the Dai-Oni; it is wondrous to look upon, save for its face which is radiant with evil. Behind it are ranged three monsters, its allies. The first is an enormous giant toad-being, slimy and warty, with a mouth almost as large as its head. The second is a giant insect, not unlike a grotesquely huge praying mantis, in plated armour of chitin, its mandibles working horribly. The third is a huge fifteen-foot man of bronze, with the legs of a goat. Its bronze skin is green and pitted with age. However, its eyes are two orbs of red flame, glowing with power.

The Dai-Oni laughs maniacally and says, 'At least you managed to reach the Place of Battle, mortal – but you will not leave it alive! These,' and it gestures at its followers, 'are my demon friends. Graalsch, devour!' it says. The enormous toad-thing hops forward. The ghostly crowd seems to roar in anticipation.

If you have no allies, turn to 254. If you do, they wait expectantly for your command. Somehow you seem to know that the rules of the Arena dictate that battles can only be between single entities. Who will you send against the toad-being? (Obviously you may send only those beings you have recorded as Allies.)

The Ki-Rin?	Turn to 146
The Sabre-toothed Tiger?	Turn to 172
Eleanor the Enchantress?	Turn to 162
The Golden Company?	Turn to 184
The Phoenix?	Turn to 194
The Tatsu?	Turn to 208
The wooden rod engraved with a serpent shape?	Turn to 228

139

After some minutes of sword-flailing, the beast pads softly away, but you daren't sleep in case it returns. Lose 2 STAMINA points for a sleepless night. Turn to **151**.

140

Lose 1 Honour point for this unheroic decision. You approach the village and creep along the wall of a house, your bow at the ready. You look into the village square. Villagers are fleeing everywhere; near by, a Samurai is robbing the body of an old man. You decide to use a willow-leaf arrow. Roll two dice: if the result is less than your SKILL, turn to **226**; if it is equal to or greater than your SKILL, turn to **240**.

141

You dive headlong into the river, your wakizashi blade clamped between your teeth, but it will do you no good here, out of your element. You are suddenly surrounded by powerful green-skinned men. The scaly monsters have vicious webbed claws which rake your body and drag you down into the murky depths. There is nothing you can do; you have fallen into the arms of the Kappa, from which there is no escape.

142

Your sword arcs down and shears through the guard's shoulder, collarbone and sternum, bursting his heart. He dies instantly in a fountain of blood.

You race on. The corridor ends in a stairwell, stairs going down and up. Will you ascend (turn to **108**) or descend (turn to **122**)?

143

The spider threshes feebly on its back in its death-throes. Beyond, you see more giant webs and burrows; to the right is a cave; behind you the water-level still rises. Will you enter the cave (turn to **91**), or hack your way through the webs (turn to **79**)?

144

The Tatsu is the one from the forest. It recognizes you and halts before you. If you have a jade amulet fashioned in the shape of a dragon, turn to **12**. If not, turn to **166**.

145

As you flee, the headman's head lifts cleanly off his shoulders and floats into the air, followed by the heads of everyone else in the village. They are Rokuro-Kubi, you realize in horror, undead whose heads detach from their bodies at night in order to hunt. The flying heads dart at you, jaws snapping viciously. You have broken through the ring of elders, but are soon faced by the heads of several of the villagers. You must fight them as if they were a single many-headed monster.

ROKURO-KUBISKILL 11 STAMINA 17

If you win, turn to **85**.

146

You order the Ki-Rin to attack. It flies into the air and swoops down towards the toad, its hoofs flashing with flames. Graalsch, the toad-being, fixes its huge eyes upon the Ki-Rin. Suddenly it opens its huge maw, leaps into the air and bites the Ki-Rin in two before it can escape. It bounds back to the ground with a meaty slap, swallowing contentedly. The Dai-Oni laughs wildly. Remove the Ki-Rin's name from your list of allies. You have no time for mourning: the toad-thing is advancing towards you. If you now have no allies left, turn to **254**. Otherwise, which ally will you send against the toad (use only those still noted on your *Adventure Sheet*):

The Sabre-toothed Tiger?	Turn to **172**
Eleanor the Enchantress?	Turn to **162**
The Golden Company?	Turn to **184**
The Phoenix?	Turn to **194**
The Tatsu?	Turn to **208**
The wooden rod engraved with a serpent shape?	Turn to **228**

147

Taking one springy step as if sauntering nonchalantly towards the peasants, your muscles suddenly tauten and propel you forward in a leap which has them gawping in astonishment. The bravest of them had been reaching for staves piled near by, but your sword-blade pierces the turf before the stack and the charcoal-burners cower in fear. The eldest of them, a crook-legged fellow, creaks painfully to

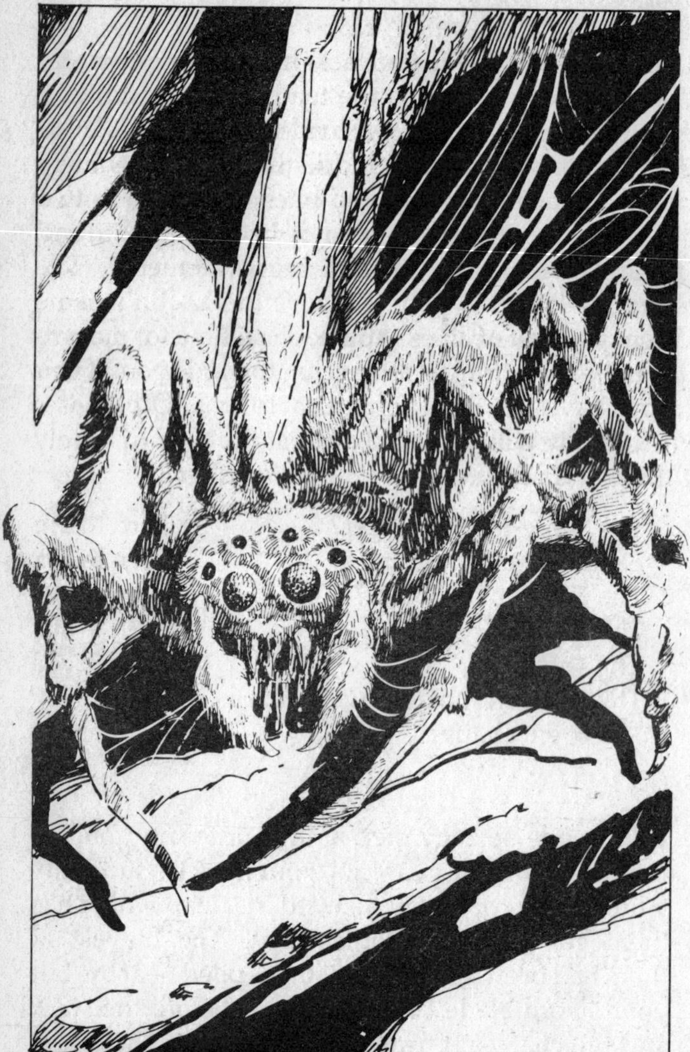

his arthritic knees and humbly begs your pardon for the insulting behaviour of his son. He offers to show you a safe village near by in which you may pass the night. Looking up to see your stern expression he begs you to take his son as a slave that you may teach him humility, but he beseeches you not to kill him. Will you make them swear an oath of allegiance before going on (turn to **163**), or command the old man and his son to show you the sanctuary of the village (turn to **179**)?

148

Wearing the guard's armour, in the colours of Lord Tsietsin, you and Moichi approach the Shikome. They stare at you blankly as you tell your tale. One of them grunts and shambles away to return with three of his fellows. They will take you to Lord Tsietsin, it growls. The three Shikome lead you into the palace, through corridors and rooms. Will you attack the guards now (turn to **256**), or let them take you to Lord Tsietsin (turn to **180**)?

149

A few gnarled trees and great holes in the ground relieve the rain-drenched land of its monotony. A curious web stretched between two trees thirty feet apart stops you in your tracks. Suddenly a flat circular slab of rock is hurled aside from the entrance of a huge burrow, and an enormous trap-door spider leaps upon you. It is taller than you and its mandibles scissor together like great scythe-blades. You must fight for your life.

TOTATE KUMO   SKILL 10   STAMINA 14

If you win, turn to **143**.

150

The Dai-Oni smiles evilly, 'Simply done, mortal.' It summons up the last of its magical powers and casts a Spell of Fortune on you. Gain 2 LUCK points. 'You will need good fortune, but even that will not be enough.' Then its body dies. If you have a jade amulet fashioned in the shape of a Tatsu, turn to **220**. If not, turn to **270**.

151

You are still sawing at the trap with your wakizashi in the morning when there is a shout behind you. The charcoal-burners have returned. Mustering as much authority as you can in the unfortunate circumstances, you order them to free you from the trap. They discuss what to do with the trapped Samurai. The most popular idea is to bury you alive inside one of the charcoal ovens. They strip bark from a nearby tree preparatory to binding you. Will you tell them of the importance of your mission (turn to **89**), or warn them they will be haunted by spirits if they kill the Shogun's champion (turn to **101**)?

152

Without hesitating, you shout 'Harmony', as loud as you can. The sound echoes like a trumpet blast through the quiet gloom of this hall of shadows. Ikiru recoils in horror on his throne. 'No!' he rasps, a sound like chalk screeching on a blackboard.

A blaze of light erupts from the sword, dispelling the shadows and causing Ikiru to cover his cowled face even further. The flare dies down as quickly as it came. Singing Death rises majestically into the air and then hurtles towards you with fantastic speed, straight into your outstretched hands, where it seems to nestle as if welcoming you.

The effect is instantaneous; you are filled with strength and well-being. Gain 2 LUCK points, 2 SKILL points and 4 STAMINA points, even if any of these bonuses takes you beyond your *Initial* status. You stand for a moment unable to act, as raw vitality courses through you. The cowled figure gestures hurriedly and a shadow form floats up out of the pit. It begins to take shape before you. It is vaguely man-like, but with a horned head and massive taloned claws. It is a Shadow Demon, only semi-corporeal, a creature from the nether regions. If your Honour is 5 or more, turn to **274**. If it is less than 5, turn to **174**.

153

The shards of bone that were the Rokuro-Kubi's skull litter the ground all around you. Though the

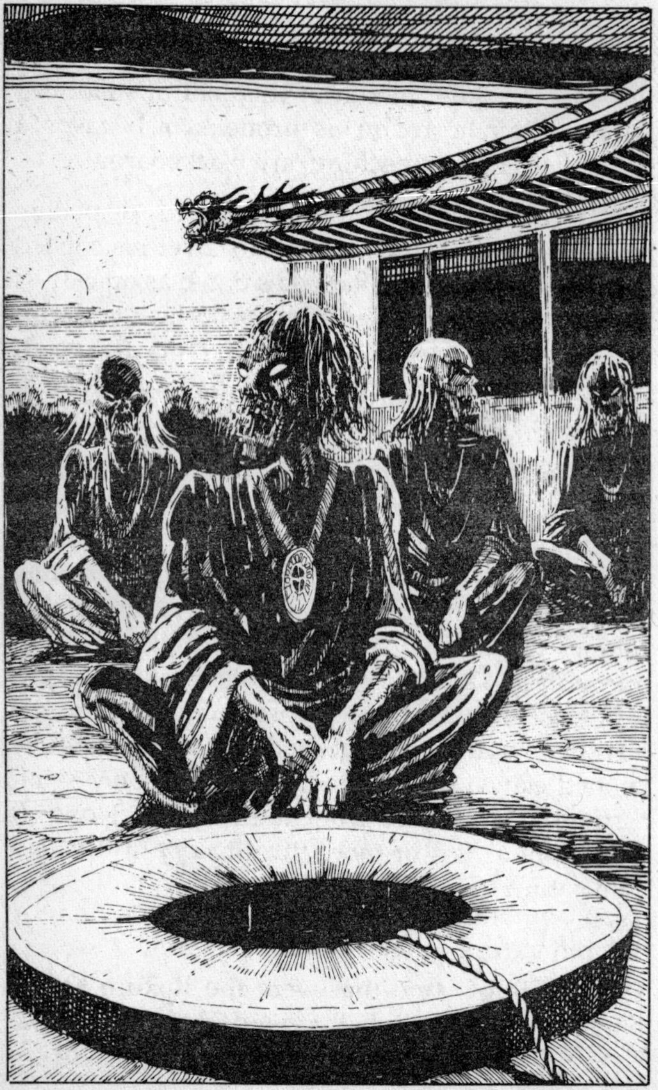

night is dark you can just see well enough to head away from the Village of the Undead. Increase your LUCK score by 1 for surviving the village. Turn to **397**.

154

The last one falls dead before you. 'Come, let me slay the rest of you,' you shout boldly. At the sight of their three dead comrades and the Shogun's champion standing resolute, the other Samurai turn tail and flee. Turn to **176**.

155

As the sun finally slips below the hills and it begins to get dark, the talk of the elders becomes slowly more and more meaningless. A strange clacking, somewhat like castanets, startles you and you see that the jaws of the headmen are snapping open and shut uncontrollably. The clacking is soon going on all around you. Will you flee in terror (turn to **145**), or wait to see if the strange fit which has seized them all passes (turn to **133**)?

156

The strange creature, its eyes glowing with baleful orange light, swoops closer, opens its mouth and breathes a thin stream of flame at you. You duck, but you cannot avoid it completely without falling off the pinnacle, and it singes you painfully. Lose 4 STAMINA points. If you are still alive, the Tatsu turns for another attack, and you decide you cannot fight it from this exposed position. You open the

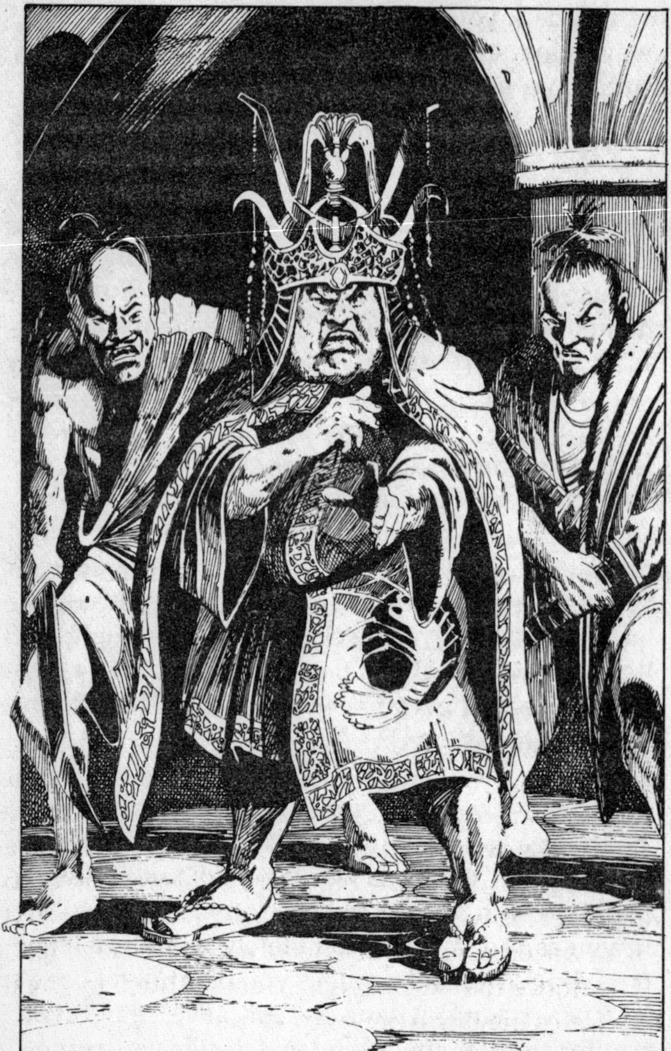

door suspended behind you and return to the Hub. Turn back to **8** and choose again, but you cannot choose an option you have already chosen.

157

There are several lines of scrawny bulrushes leading away from the place to which you have retraced your steps. So far you have been able to follow them through the muddy waters, but now you don't know which line borders the path. You choose wrong and step into a bottomless pool of mud. The more you struggle the faster you are pulled under and the quagmire swallows you up. Ikiru's reign will spread to all of Hachiman.

158

You run down a long corridor and soon find yourself lost in a maze of corridors and rooms, mostly empty save for servants and slaves, who stare at you in amazement. You are rounding a corner when you are greeted by a sight that causes you to pull up short in surprise. You have bumped into Lord Tsietsin himself, waddling down the corridor towards you, two Samurai at either side. Lord Tsietsin is a large fat man with great blubbery jaws and a face wreathed in fat. Two pig-like eyes flare at you in outrage. He wears a voluminous kimono, bedecked with an enormous robe, adorned with gold leaf. You notice that he is openly wearing the hat which indicates the office of Shogun.

Tsietsin gasps in fear as he recognizes you, signals to his guards, turns around and lumbers away from you. The Samurai draw their blades, bow and dash to the attack. Turn to **302**.

159

As soon as you increase your pace, your feet slip out from under you on the treacherous green slime. *Test your Luck*, but add 1 to the die roll because you are crossing the ford heedless of the danger. If you are Lucky, turn to **283**. If you are Unlucky, turn to **323**.

160

'But, my lord, who would believe such as I could hold captive one as noble as yourself!' Moichi exclaims. You stare at him suspiciously for a moment before ordering him to get on with it. You give your weapons to Moichi. He grabs you around the neck and frogmarches you forward. You cannot help but feel that Moichi is enjoying this.

The two Shikome stare at you with dull expressions, as Moichi tells them your story. One of the guards grunts, and grins at you horribly before shambling away. He returns with three of his friends, all as ugly and malodorous as one another. These three lead you into the palace. One of them grunts at Moichi, 'More sport for the master, eh?' and gives you a vicious kick in the ribs. Lose 2 STAMINA points. 'Yes, he is to be horribly tortured,' says Moichi, leering at you. You glare back. Will you wait until you have been taken before Tsietsin (turn to **180**), or have Moichi let you go so that you can both attack the Shikome guards (turn to **204**)?

161

Thirstily you bend your mouth to the refreshing pool and drink deeply of the Waters of Knowledge. Enlightenment floods your being. Suddenly you know the answer to everything: it is as if you are a god. So sublime is the experience that you cannot contain yourself and drink lustily once more. You are intoxicated with knowledge, the knowledge of alchemists, the knowledge of the meadow wren, the knowledge of the wisest scholars of the court and much more. Your thirst for knowledge is unquenched and you drink on, but you are still unsated: you throw yourself into the pool to immerse yourself fully in knowledge and, intoxicated, you drown.

162

You order Eleanor to fight the toad. She runs forward, blue energy crackling at her fingertips, but the Toad Demon leaps forward with incredible speed and, before she can do anything, snaps her up in its great maw in one great gulp. She is no more. You step back in horror. Remove her name from the list of allies on your *Adventure Sheet*. If you now have no allies left, turn to **254**. Otherwise, which ally will you send against the toad? Use only those still noted on your *Adventure Sheet*:

The Ki-Rin?	Turn to **146**
The Phoenix?	Turn to **194**
The wooden rod engraved with a serpent shape?	Turn to **228**

163

They repeat the oath of allegiance and you inform them that it is the Shogun's wish that clemency be shown to his subjects and that you will spare their lives. Increase your Honour by 1. Will you command the old man to show you to the sanctuary of the village (turn to **179**), or journey on alone (turn to **195**)?

164

The arrow flies true and thuds into the thing's chest. It staggers back, but there is no appreciable effect. You loose another, but it goes straight through its legs, between two bones. The other skeletons are almost on the bridge now. You have no more time. Turn to **242**.

165

You ask the silver Samurai's advice as you set out on the path to the statue of Hammurabi, but he remains tight-lipped and silent. Once again the magician appears out of thin air and the statue of the Lord of the Flies flexes his forty-foot wings and turns his giant, glinting, multi-faceted eyes upon you. There is a loud buzzing all around you and swarms of flies begin to attack your eyes and skin. Hammurabi's servants have come to protect him. The swarm is soon inches thick all over you; you choke helplessly and then Hammurabi strikes. It seems he has decided your head will make a tasty morsel, and you are powerless to stop him.

166

It speaks in a thunderous voice, 'You thought you had slain me, but I am far more powerful than you could ever have imagined, mortal.' The Tatsu, eyes glowing with baleful orange light, swoops closer, opens its mouth and breathes a thin stream of flame at you. You duck, but you cannot avoid it completely without falling off the pinnacle, and it singes you painfully. Lose 4 STAMINA points. The Tatsu turns for another attack. You decide you cannot fight from this exposed position. You open the door suspended behind you and return to the Hub. Turn back to 8 and choose again, but you cannot choose an option you have chosen already.

167

It is the work of only two minutes to divest yourself of the armour. Summoning all your strength, you hurl it piece by piece over to the other bank. To your consternation a scaly green arm reaches up out of the water, catches the breastplate in mid-air and descends gently below the surface. You have lost your breastplate. Will you plunge into the river to try to get it back (turn to **141**), or race to the pier of rock, keeping to the side nearest the white water (turn to **127**)?

168

You step out into bright sunshine. The courtyard is full of busy people – tradesmen, craftsmen, soldiers and so on – and none of them pays any heed to you as you saunter boldly towards the gate. You walk through as if intent on some mission and no one questions your actions. Marvelling at your good fortune, you hurry on to the main road. There you head north, towards the Forest of Shadows. Soon you pass between two wooded hills making a shallow valley. Turn to **386**.

169

There are several lines of scrawny bulrushes leading away from the place to which you have retraced your steps. So far you have been able to follow them through the muddy waters, but now you don't know which line marks the edge of the path. Boldly you set off along one of the lines and soon you are within sight of the low hill, which is curtained by sheets of driving rain. As the ground slopes up and you leave the rising waters behind you notice that all the creatures of the swamp – rats, marsh salamanders and even a giant dragon-newt, which seems too scared to think about gobbling you up – are racing towards the same patch of high ground to escape the flood. Turn to **149**.

170

You decide to use bowel-raker arrows as they are the most deadly. You draw and aim your bow at the nearest Shikome. Roll two dice. If you throw less than your SKILL, turn to **232**. If you throw equal to or more than your SKILL, turn to **244**.

171

At the last moment you bring the sword-blade down towards the green water in a slashing motion which slices through the net. Then you lunge again with scarcely believable speed. Your sword-point buries itself in the face of the scaly green monster, which turns purple and sinks below the surface, bubbling purplish blood. The second is still surging towards the ford and you just have time to reach the other bank, teetering dangerously every step of the way. Turn to **395**.

172

The tiger races forward and roars menacingly; the toad-thing hops back uncertainly. Graalsch, the Toad Demon, snaps its head forward to strike, its great maw snapping, but the huge tiger dodges aside, moving with incredible swiftness and lays open the toad's side with a sweep of one of its great taloned claws. Then it proceeds to rip and tear the wailing Graalsch into shreds. After its task is completed, the tiger leaps into the air and then fades out of existence as if it had jumped to another plane. Remove it from the list of allies on your *Adventure Sheet*. The Dai-Oni bellows in rage and shouts, 'K'rllk, slay the man-thing!' and the Mantis Demon scuttles forward. If you are alone now, turn to **266**. Otherwise, which ally will you send against it (use only those still noted on your *Adventure Sheet*):

The Ki-Rin?	Turn to **278**
The Golden Company?	Turn to **304**
The Tatsu?	Turn to **294**

173

One of the scaly green monsters throws a trident as you turn to flee. *Test your Luck*. If you are Lucky, turn to **225**. If you are Unlucky, turn to **257**.

174

You must fight the Shadow Demon. Singing Death does not seem affected by its insubstantiality – it will cut shadows as well as flesh.

SHADOW DEMON   SKILL 9   STAMINA 10

If you win, turn to **212**.

175

She does not answer. You turn round to look at her, and she stares at you with a strange intensity. Her teeth start to chatter in a most unnerving way, as if she were trying to speak, but could not. At last she forces out the words, 'Go . . . Leave the village.' If you think this is scant thanks for your help and stay to eat the gruel and sleep, turn to **203**. If instead you quit the village, turn to **15**.

176

The villagers run out of their houses and their hiding-places, some shouting joyfully, others weeping over lost friends and relatives. As many villagers see to dousing the fires, a number of elders approach you. Bowing low, one of them says, 'I am Ninji, the headman. We cannot thank you enough for your noble act. Hachiman has fallen on bad times, but at least someone still follows the old ways. Here, my lord, please accept this gift.' And he hands you a silken red headband patterned with a black three-spoked wheel. 'This is the headband of

Shinmen, the legendary hero of Hachiman, who came from this village. This headband has been with us for centuries.' You feel honoured – Shinmen was a great hero. Gain 1 Honour and 1 LUCK point.

Just then a commotion starts near by: there are cries of anger and hate. A group of villagers have found a wounded Samurai raider and are dragging him towards you. They are chanting, 'Kill, kill, kill, kill.' The headman bows to you and says, 'Please rid us of this vile murderer, lord.' The Samurai lies before you, defenceless, a slim young man with a blood-stained head bandage. He looks at you defiantly, resolved not to show fear. Will you kill the Samurai as the villagers wish (turn to **238**), or spare his life (turn to **250**)?

177

Instead of bedding down for the night, you walk out of the house and into the village. The meeting of the elders is about to begin outside the headman's house. It is getting dark. Will you quit the village (turn to **15**), or join the elders (turn to **319**)?

178

'Spare me, great warrior, please spare me,' gabbles Tsietsin. 'It was Ikiru: he forced me to turn against the rightful Shogun, forgive me, I shall be his loyal vassal from now on.' This is all a tissue of transparent lies. As you look down, feeling only contempt and loathing, Tsietsin's eyes narrow in cunning malice. His right hand flicks through the air. A needle-like dagger flies from his hand and into your thigh. Lose 3 STAMINA points. If you live, you stagger back in surprise, while he lurches to his feet, drawing his sword. 'Curse you, you swine,' he cries and slashes at you. You must fight Lord Tsietsin.

LORD TSIETSIN   SKILL 7   STAMINA 11

If you win, turn to **322**.

179

Ordering the old man to show you the way alone, you leave the charcoal-burners' woods. He bids farewell to his son, then fawningly ushers you on. He takes you along a winding track that leads to the dales of Kanshuro, a land where wooded plateaux are riven by beautiful and peaceful dales, which nestle unseen between cliffs cut into the limestone by the rivers which formed them. At dusk you take a path down into the Vale of Tinshu to a small and picturesque village. You turn to the old man to ask its name, but he has fallen to the ground. You try to rouse him but his heart has stopped. He is dead. Turn to **5**.

180

You are taken into the audience-room of the palace, where you soon realize you have made a mistake. Lord Tsietsin, a fat, pig-like man, sits before you, but the walls are lined with Samurai warriors, over sixty of them including many Shikome. One of the guards recognizes you from the village, and within moments you and Moichi have been sliced into bits by their swords.

181

The water-level rises faster and faster and it becomes harder and harder to retrace your steps on the safe path across the featureless fens. At any moment you could step off the path and be swallowed up by the stinking quagmires. *Test your Luck*. If you are Lucky, turn to **169**. If you are Unlucky, turn to **157**.

182

You open the iron war-fan. It reveals a beautiful image painted on its spread blades, an insignia you do not recognize, something very ancient: nine gold arrow fletches pointing inward to a blue circle, the whole set on a plain white background. Puzzled, you fold it up and place it in your backpack. Will you put on the helmet, if you have not already done so (turn to **210**), drink from the bottle, if you have not already done so (turn to **196**), or leave the cavern (turn to **222**)?

183

With your back to the tree, you direct a fresh onslaught. Desperate measures are called for if you are to avoid death at the hands of the scaly green monsters. Will you try a trick suggested by the element brimstone (turn to **231**), has the thought of their strange flat-topped heads entered your mind (turn to **255**), or will you pretend to be about to cast a spell on them (turn to **277**)?

184

The Knights of the Golden Company utter a battle-cry and charge forward with military precision. However, their weapons, straight swords and maces, make little impression on the leathery skin of the Toad Demon. Graalsch lays about itself with ferocious accuracy; each super-fast dart of its head bites a knight in two. Within moments they are all dead. You stand aghast at its horrible power. Remove the knights from the list of allies on your *Adventure Sheet*. Graalsch turns upon you and hops forward. If you are now without allies, turn to **254**. Otherwise which ally will you commit now (use only those listed on your *Adventure Sheet*):

The Tatsu?	Turn to **208**
The Sabre-toothed Tiger?	Turn to **172**
The Ki-Rin?	Turn to **146**

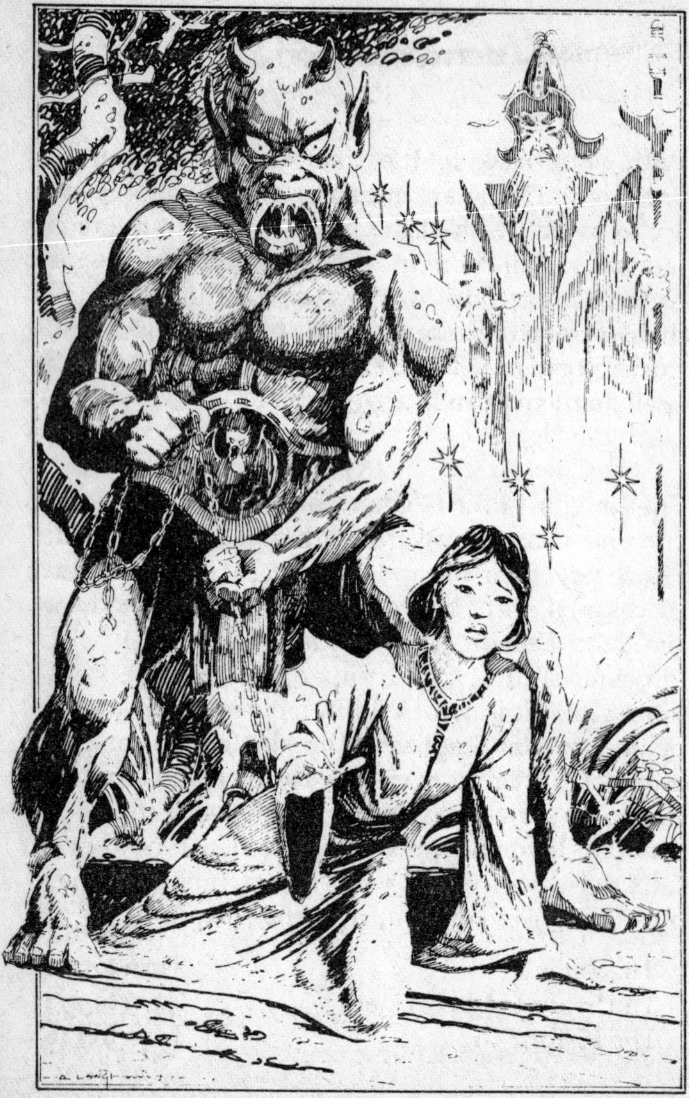

185

The silver Samurai strides purposefully at your side towards the twin statues of the demon and captive priestess. The magician appears again out of thin air and the two statues – the black-skinned, red-tusked demon and the pale skinned priestess – come to life. She kneels at your feet imploring you to save her from the Pit of Demons, but her captor yanks the chain cruelly and she is pulled to the floor. The silver Samurai gives the Battle-cry of Ages and the demon is stricken with terror. They battle mightily but even the eldritch powers of the demon are as naught against the flashing Samurai. The demon is slain. The chain disappears and the silver Samurai melts into a little silver puddle. The priestess puts her hand in yours. 'Whither now, gallant saviour?' Will you take the path to the statue of the Sea Dragon (turn to **55**) or to the statue of Hammurabi, Lord of the Flies (turn to **75**)?

186

You take out the war-fan. The knight gasps in surprise. 'You have it!' he exclaims. You hand it to him and then he kneels before you, the other knights following suit.

'When you travel to the Place of Battle, we shall be there to fight at your side. Long have we sought this artefact.'

Suddenly you find yourself back at the Hub surrounded by stars and the eight doors. Note that the

Golden Company are your allies. Return to **8** and choose again, but you cannot choose an option you have tried already.

187

You head hastily in the opposite direction to that by which you entered the village. Nobody appears to notice you leave and you begin to breathe easier. Suddenly you catch sight of the old charcoal-burner who brought you to the village. You thought him quite dead, having left his unbreathing corpse at the other edge of the village, yet here he is grinning at you from behind a wall. You step forward, but stop as his head sails up into the night air: another Rokuro-Kubi! It spits black gobbets of poison which hiss and smoke as they spatter against your face. You are in agony. Lose 2 STAMINA points. You must fight the Rokuro-Kubi as it flies through the air snapping viciously.

ROKURO-KUBI   SKILL 7   STAMINA 8

If you win, turn to **153**.

188
The Dai-Oni smiles evilly. 'Simply defeat him in battle, mortal.' He laughs wildly, before his body dies. If you have a jade amulet fashioned in the shape of a Tatsu, turn to **220**. If not, turn to **270**.

189
Suddenly, Singing Death flares brightly once more and the bolts of dark energy simply cease to be, extinguished in its bright light. Ikiru staggers back, but the light fades as quickly as it sprang up. Turn to **199**.

190
The last one falls dead at your feet. You expect another to step forward and take his place, but none of the other Samurai makes a move. The villagers cower in their homes, watching the proceedings with fear and hope in their eyes. One or two of the Samurai shuffle back uncomfortably. They have been awed by your swordsmanship.

One of them says, 'You are a master of the sword and you have won great honour here. As you have fought so well, we will leave now and spare your life.' His words sound courteous, but you sense it is fear of facing you rather than the desire to honour you that is making them leave. They leave the village as fast as they can; you feel too tired to pursue them. Gain 1 Honour point for your challenge and your defence of the village. Turn to **176**.

191

She places her hand on your shoulder, points to the gruel and the mattress, then hurries away into her own little bedroom while the sun turns the sky red as it sets. If you wish to leave the house after finishing the repair, turn to **177**. If you eat and sleep, turn to **203**.

192

The arrow flies true and thuds into its chest. The undead Samurai shrieks horribly and falls to the ground. There it begins to dissolve, as does the arrow, until there is nothing left but ash. As it does so, the skeletons fall back into the river and sink from sight. The redness fades from the river and the sky lightens.

You walk across the bridge, and inspect the heap of ash. Among the ashes you notice an ivory horn of fine workmanship inlaid with silver tracery depicting a sabre-toothed tiger. You pick it up and walk on. Turn to **211**.

193

On close inspection the river looks quite deep and you will not be able to cross wearing your heavy armour. If you wish to hurl the armour to the other side before plunging in, turn to **167**. If you prefer to risk the ford, will you cross near the frothing white water (turn to **213**) or near the green depths on the upstream side where you are now (turn to **201**)?

194

You order the Phoenix to attack Graalsch the Toad Demon. The Phoenix flies straight at the toad-thing. Oddly, Graalsch does not move, even when the Phoenix turns into a fireball almost on top of it. When the flames die, Graalsch is completely unhurt, as if it were immune to flames of any sort. The toad-thing's head darts forward and its huge maw closes around the magical bird, swallowing it up in one gulp. The Phoenix is no more. Remove its name from the list of allies on your *Adventure Sheet*. If you now have no allies left, turn to **254**. Otherwise, which ally will you send against the toad (use only those still noted on your *Adventure Sheet*):

The Ki-Rin?	Turn to **146**
Eleanor the Enchantress?	Turn to **162**
The wooden rod engraved with a serpent shape?	Turn to **228**

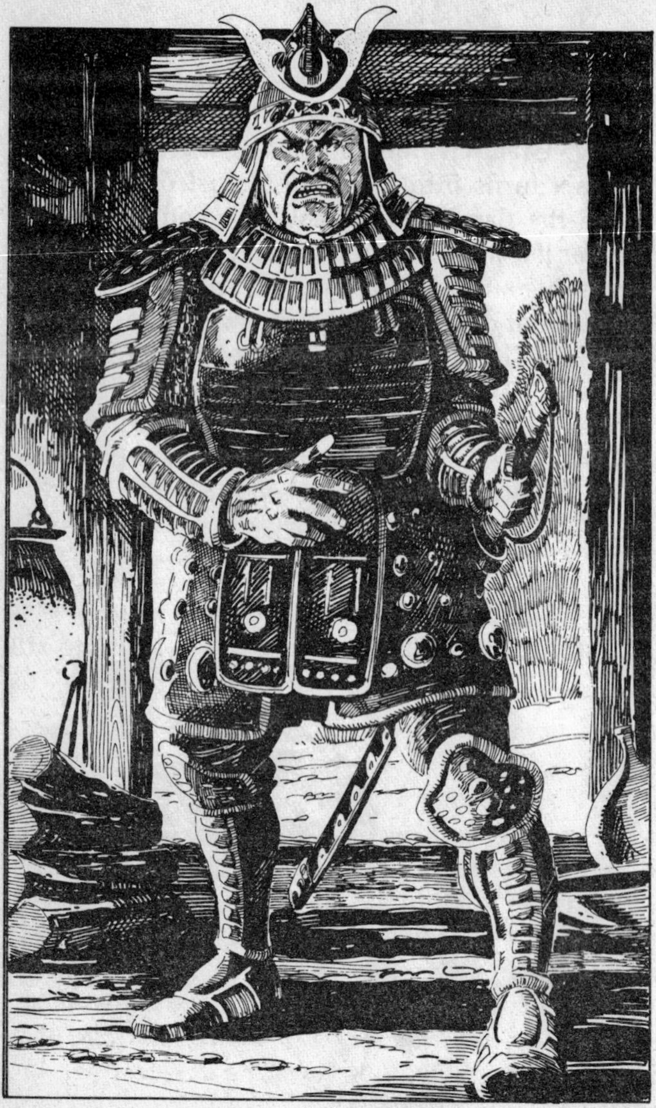

195

The road forks behind the charcoal-burners' wood and you decide to take the left fork, which drops out of sight into a small wooded dale. As you descend, dusk draws in and the sight of a fire outside a goatherd's rough hut is welcoming. You march closer to see if it offers shelter for the night, when a figure dressed in the lacquered armour of a Samurai stoops beneath the low doorway and walks to the fire. The flames illuminate his golden armour and the proud face is unmistakable. It is Yoro Ginsei, erstwhile captain of the executed Lord Toda's guard. Toda plotted against the Shogun. His disgraced Samurai committed seppuku, killing themselves rather than suffering dishonour, but Ginsei decided to live on as a ronin, a Samurai without a lord. His hatred of Samurai is well known. Turn to **209**.

196

You raise the bottle to your lips and a vile stench fills your nostrils. You sip it – the taste makes you heave and retch, but the liquid burns down your throat. It is invigorating and health-giving; the liquid is healing some of your wounds. Regain up to 3 points of lost STAMINA. There is enough liquid left for one good drink – you may drink it at any time to restore up to 5 points of STAMINA. Will you open the war-fan, if you have not already done so (turn to **182**), put on the helmet, if you have not already done so (turn to **210**), or leave the cavern (turn to **222**)?

197

With a single almighty bound you have leapt out of the clutches of the Groundhog on to the rock-shelf beyond. Will you run into the cave (turn to **265**), or climb to the crest and escape (turn to **259**)?

198

The knights run forward with military precision. Twin bolts of ruby fire leap from the eyes of Gargantus and strike one of the knights, who is hurled forty feet through the air and killed. The other knights are not using their swords and maces; instead they are wielding lengths of rope. They run around Gargantus's legs, dodging and weaving and casting their lassoed ropes at Gargantus. Soon they have his arms enmeshed, and one of his legs; but two men lie dead. Then the remaining knights all pull on the ropes and Gargantus slowly begins to topple. He gives a great cry of despair, like the roar of a huge waterfall, before crashing to the ground. As soon as he touches the earth, the light fades from his eyes and he lies inert, nothing but a massive bronze statue. The leader of the Golden Company says to you, 'Our duty has been discharged, bearer of the war-fan. Farewell.' Then they literally step away into nothingness.

The Dai-One speaks, 'You have done well, mortal, but now I shall kill you.' It advances, wielding a massive spiked iron club, a Tetsubo. If you still have the Ki-Rin as an ally, you may send it against the Dai-Oni (turn to **394**). Otherwise, you will have to fight the Dai-Oni alone (turn to **292**).

199

A sword of black steel, etched with glowing red runes, appears in Ikiru's shadowy grasp and you both fall to combat, dark against light. Each time you hit him, deduct STAMINA as usual, but also *Test your Luck*. If you are Lucky, turn to **235**. If you are Unlucky, just fight on. Each time Ikiru hits you, not only do you lose the normal STAMINA, but a powerful surge of force erupts from his black runesword and threatens to overcome you. Roll two dice: if the result is more than your STAMINA, turn to **47**; if it is not, fight on.

IKIRU   SKILL 12   STAMINA 12

If you win, turn to **400**.

200

The knight's face falls when he sees you have no idea what he is referring to. 'Another wanderer that does not bring us what we seek,' he mutters. 'Begone! We will not aid you. May the Demon Lord devour you!' With that you find yourself back at the Hub, surrounded by stars and the eight doors. Return to **8** and choose again, but you cannot choose an option you have already tried.

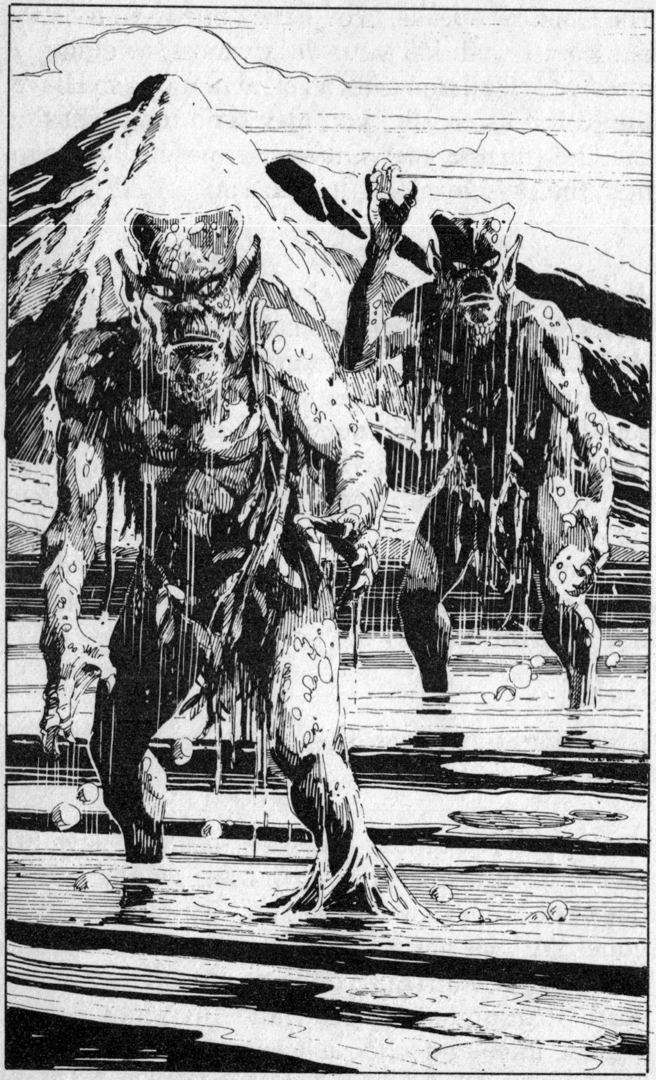

201

Choosing the side of the ford nearest the green depths, you cautiously feel your way towards the far bank across the pier of rock, which is only inches below the surface of the river. The green slime which covers the rock is treacherous underfoot. Suddenly two figures rise majestically out of the depths. They have scaly green skins and curious flat-topped heads. They move as if balancing something invisible on top of their heads, but they also have dangerous-looking webbed claws, and they are surging towards the ford. Will you lunge your sword at the nearest (turn to **233**), or try to make a dash for the far bank (turn to **159**)?

202

One of the Samurai sees his comrade's dead body and shouts a warning. You dart into cover, but are spotted, and three Samurai rush forward. One of them recognizes you and says, 'The Shogun's – sorry, the *ex*-Shogun's champion. Kill the mangy, flea-ridden goat!' They come at you in a rush, wildly brandishing their swords. You must fight them all at once. If you have the skill of Karumijutsu, you may subtract 1 from all their Attack Rolls for this combat only, as you jump and leap over them, trying to dodge their blows.

	SKILL	STAMINA
First SAMURAI	6	7
Second SAMURAI	8	8
Third SAMURAI	7	6

If you kill all three of them, turn to **154**.

203

It is peaceful and calm in the village as you take off your armour, bed down and drift off to sleep . . . There is a sudden sharp pain in your leg. You sit bolt upright to see by the light of the moon a disembodied head feeding off your leg. It is the head of the peasant woman. There is no blood at the severed neck, and with a thrill of horror you realize she is a Rokuro-Kubi, an undead being whose head detaches itself from its body at night in order to hunt. You have already lost 3 STAMINA points. Seizing your katana, you give battle to the floating head, which snaps at you viciously.

ROKURO-KUBI   SKILL 8   STAMINA 8

If you win, turn to **187**.

204

You grab your swords from Moichi and leap to the attack, as does your retainer. The Shikome are completely surprised. They may not fight back for two rounds of combat. Moichi is fighting one, but you must fight the other two.

	SKILL	STAMINA
First SHIKOME	6	6
Second SHIKOME	7	5

If they are still alive after six rounds of combat, turn to **218**. If you have slain them before then, turn to **336**.

205

All goes still for a moment as you wedge yourself in the cave mouth, then there is a dull rumbling from the earth and the ground starts to shake once more. The tremor is a strong one and there is a great cracking noise above you. You look up in time to see a hundred tons of slate dropping from the cave roof. There is no escape: you are squashed flat.

206

The Dai-Oni screws up its face in pain and rage. 'Curse you, mortal. The secret is "Harmony". Utter that word and Singing Death will come to life and fly into your hands, but only for those of noble heart – which is why Ikiru has been unable to use it yet,' he adds with a laugh of malicious glee. Then his body dies. If you have a jade amulet fashioned in the shape of a Tatsu, turn to **220**. If not, turn to **270**.

207

Which type of arrow did you select to fire at the youth? Was it a willow-leaf arrow (turn to **223**) or a bowel-raker (turn to **239**)?

208

You order the Tatsu to the attack. It gallops into the air. Graalsch shifts its bulk to face the Tatsu, just as the dragon breathes a stream of flame that engulfs the Toad Demon. But incredibly, as the flames subside, it becomes apparent that Graalsch is completely unhurt. As the Tatsu pauses momentarily in surprise, the Toad Demon executes a great bound into the air and bites the Tatsu's head clean off its shoulders. The Tatsu's body simply fades out of existence. Remove its name from your list of allies. The Dai-Oni mocks you at this point and orders Graalsch on. If you are without allies now, turn to **254**. Otherwise, which ally will you send against the toad (use only those still noted on your *Adventure Sheet*):

The Ki-Rin?	Turn to **146**
The Golden Company?	Turn to **184**
The Sabre-toothed Tiger?	Turn to **172**

209

The ronin catches sight of you against the skyline and, hand on the hilt of his katana, he swaggers towards you. He is a traitor and an enemy of your lord, but a peerless swordsman. Will you hide among the trees (turn to 221), or wait to see what Ginsei will do (turn to 241)?

210

Gingerly you place the silvered helmet on your head. For a moment nothing happens, but then lancing bolts of pain lacerate your brain. You scream in agony and rip the helmet off your head. However, your brain feels slightly numb, as if you weren't quite yourself. It is a Helmet of Befuddlement (lose 1 SKILL point). You may take the helmet with you in any case, if you so wish. Will you drink from the bottle, if you have not already done so (turn to 196), open the war-fan, if you have not already done so (turn to 182), or leave the cavern (turn to 222)?

211

You follow the road to the mountains and the lair of Ikiru. The day passes uneventfully and you spend the night under the stars. You rise the next day, refreshed. You may restore up to 2 STAMINA points. You press on, leaving the road, until you come to the Shios'ii Mountains. A goat-track climbs up one of the largest mountains and you decide to follow it. Turn to 8.

212

The Shadow Demon is dead and Ikiru hisses in rage and fear. Hurriedly he raises his hands high and utters a strange cry. Shapes begin to rise up out of the pit and form around him, a phalanx of guardian shadows. A score surround him in moments.

Will you step forward and throw Singing Death into the pit (turn to 312)? Will you wait to see what happens (turn to 51)? Will you walk around the pit and try to stride boldly through the shadowy forms (turn to 298)? Or will you throw Singing Death like a spear at Ikiru (turn to 63)?

213

Choosing the side of the ford nearest the frothing white waters, you cautiously feel your way towards the far bank across the pier of rock, which is only inches below the surface of the river. The green slime is treacherous underfoot and it is all you can do to keep your balance. Suddenly two scaly green figures rise up out of the green depths upstream and begin to wade towards the ford. They have webbed claws and curiously shaped flat-topped heads. Will you make a dash for the far bank (turn to 159), draw back from the ford and try to find a safer place to cross (turn to 245), or give battle on the ford itself (turn to 315)?

214

You hold up the ruby and it flashes in the sunlight, but the sabre-toothed tiger continues to hurtle towards you. Then it leaps. You must fight the tiger.

SABRE-TOOTHED
  TIGER   SKILL 10   STAMINA 12

If you win, there is nothing more here, so you step back through the door to the Hub. Return to **8** and choose again, but not an option you have already tried.

215

It does not take you long to find a suitable plank and nail it to the screen. At least the little house will be warmer to live in now. To your consternation, the melancholic old woman becomes agitated while you work, and her teeth begin to chatter like castanets. Will you ignore her and finish work (turn to **191**), or ask her what is wrong (turn to **175**)?

216

You dart from house to house, completely unseen. You manage to kill another Samurai with an arrow in the chest. The others turn round in astonishment, but are unable to see their assailant. You continue your accurate archery – soon you have killed four of them and they still have not found you. This is too much for them and the remaining Samurai turn to flee. (You may recover most of the arrows, but some are broken: you will lose 1 willow-leaf, 1 armour-piercer and 1 bowel-raker.) Turn to **176**.

217

The path winds through the mist for several miles further than the map led you to expect, and you still have not caught sight of the scarlet pagoda. If you wish to turn back to the giant's causeway, turn to **113**. If not, turn to **369**.

218

The sounds of battle have alerted the others. A troop of Shikome and Samurai appear on the scene and it is not long before you and Moichi have been overpowered. Moichi is slain out of hand, but they take you prisoner, making gibes about the Shogun and his champion as they do so – they plainly know who you are. You are filled with sorrow at the loss of your loyal retainer.

You are unceremoniously thrown into a small cell in the palace dungeon. The gaoler, a large beefy man in a stained leather jerkin, says jeeringly, 'You will be taken before the Shogun Tsietsin on the morrow.' He then slams the massive, iron-studded, oaken door of the cell in your face.

You are alone. They have taken your swords, and it is this rather than the cruel gibes and the indignity of capture that fills you with shame. Lose 1 Honour point for their loss. There is nothing you can do but wait for the morning, so you lie down on the wooden pallet in the corner and go to sleep. Turn to **316**.

219

The oldest of the charcoal-burners catches up with you after a time and fawningly begs that he may show you to a place of safety so that it may not be said that his family dishonoured a Samurai. He takes you along a winding track that leads to the vales of Kanshuro where wooded plateaux are riven by beautiful and peaceful dales, which nestle unseen between cliffs cut into the limestone by the rivers which formed them. At dusk you take a path down into the Vale of Tinshu to a small and picturesque village. You turn to the old man to ask its name, but he has fallen to the ground. You try to rouse him but his heart has stopped. He is dead. Turn to **5**.

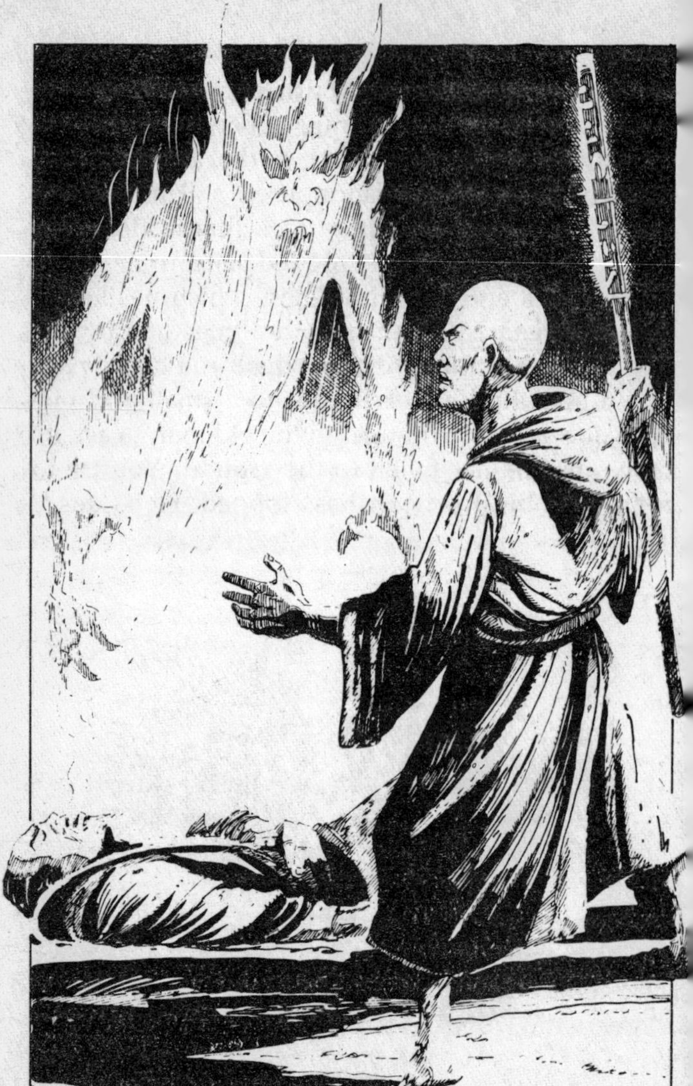

220

A terrible thing happens. Out of the body of the Dai-Oni a spectral shape coalesces, a ghostly form of the demon, with insubstantial taloned hands. It is a Shura, or warrior ghost, the spirit of the Dai-Oni come to avenge its death.

But you remember the words of the Tatsu and invoke the Jizo of Demons, saying, 'A Shura is here, O Jizo. Come and execute your purpose.'

As you finish the word 'purpose', a being appears before you. He is dressed as a warrior monk and bears a staff inscribed with glowing runes. You are filled with awe at the sight of it. The Jizo of Demons ignores you and merely strikes the ghostly spectre. The apparition promptly disappears with an echoing wail of dread. The Jizo, without even acknowledging your presence, also departs. Turn to **76**.

221

Ginsei calls challenges to you, but he cannot track you down. Slipping away, you reflect that it would have been a close battle. Fear wakens in your breast; you did not dare to challenge the enemy of your lord. Your honour is besmirched; you feel unworthy to be the Shogun's champion. Subtract 2 from your Honour. Night is falling and you try to find a dry spot in the woods to sleep. Turn to **371**.

222

The exit tunnel curls upward until you can see a small circle of light ahead from a cave entrance under a rocky overhang on a hillside. The hill slopes down into a shallow valley with a road running its length. It is the main road. You must follow it north to reach Onikaru and Ikiru. Turn to **386**.

223

The willow-leaf arrow whistles through the air and buries itself in the youth's side: he screams and doubles up in agony. One of the charcoal-burners tries to grab a stave, but two others restrain him and the eldest of them throws himself at your feet, imploring you not to kill his son. Looking up and seeing your stern countenance, he offers to take you to a village where you may pass the night safely. Will you command him to take you to the village (turn to **253**), or walk on alone (turn to **195**)?

224

You aim and fire. If you are successful, you may deduct the total damage-value of your arrow from the tiger's STAMINA of 12. You have the chance to fire three arrows before it is upon you. You must fight it now.

SABRE-TOOTHED
  TIGER   SKILL 10   STAMINA 12

If you win, there is nothing more here, so you step back through the door to the Hub. Return to **8** and choose again, but not an option you have already tried.

225

The trident catches in a low branch and you are able to make good your escape. Turn to **245**.

226

You draw and fire: the arrow skewers his neck. He throws up his arms and falls dead. (You will not be able to retrieve this arrow, so cross off a willow-leaf arrow from your *Adventure Sheet*.) Now *Test your Luck*. If you are Lucky, turn to **216**. If you are Unlucky, turn to **202**.

227

The road runs down to the river's edge at a ford. You can see, running to the other bank just below the surface, a pier of rock, over which the river pours like a weir. Below the weir the water is white and frothy; above it is still, deep and green. The pier is ten feet wide and covered in green slime. Will you cross near the frothing white water (turn to **213**) or near the green depths upstream (turn to **201**)? Otherwise you may plunge in above the weir and swim (turn to **193**).

228

You throw the carved rod in the path of the toad-thing. Suddenly a great Serpent rears in its place and Graalsch, the Toad Demon, hesitates in fear for a moment. The serpent's great coils writhe forward and envelop the toad in a grip of steel, ever tightening, its fanged head continually diving at Graalsch's trapped body and biting into it. The Toad Demon wails horribly as the life is crushed and torn out of it. When its work is done, the serpent fades into nothingness, as if it had slithered away to another plane. Remove its name from your list of allies on your *Adventure Sheet*.

The Dai-Oni bellows in rage, 'K'rllk, slay the man-thing!' And the Mantis Demon scuttles forward. If you are now without allies, turn to **266**. Otherwise, which ally will you send against it (use only those still noted on your *Adventure Sheet*):

The Ki-Rin?	Turn to **278**
The Phoenix?	Turn to **320**
Eleanor the Enchantress?	Turn to **330**

229

The water rises faster and faster and still the bulrushes march on across the featureless expanse of fen. You are forced to swim, but after swimming many miles you are utterly exhausted and sink quietly beneath the surface to drown.

230

You run into the palace and down a long corridor

and soon find yourself lost in a maze of corridors and rooms, mostly empty except for servants and slaves, who stare at you in amazement. On rounding a corner you are greeted by a sight that causes you to stop dead in your tracks. You have almost bumped into Lord Tsietsin himself, waddling down the corridor, a Samurai at either side. Lord Tsietsin is a large fat man with great blubbery jaws and a face wreathed in fat. Two pig-like eyes flare in outrage. He wears a voluminous kimono, bedecked with an enormous robe, adorned with gold leaf. He is quite openly wearing the hat indicating the title of Shogun.

Tsietsin gasps in fear as he recognizes you, signals to his guards and lumbers away. The Samurai draw their blades, bow and then rush to the attack. Moichi darts forward and engages one. You must fight the other.

| TSIETSIN'S BODYGUARD | SKILL 9 | STAMINA 8 |

If you win, turn to 354.

231

Unfortunately you have no brimstone with which you can attack or scare the monsters. They are forcing you back to the river-bank. Your sword flashes through the air, creating the illusion of a magical barrier of blades, but at last one of the creatures gets through your guard. You are knocked to the ground and dragged into the river. You have fallen into the clutches of the Kappa, from which there is no escape.

232

With two swift and accurate shots you have killed both Shikome, who slump silently before the palace gates. Moichi's jaw drops in amazement, 'Such skill, you are truly a master of the Way of the Bow and the Sword, my lord!' This time you can detect no sarcasm in his voice. Quickly you race into the palace as quietly as possible, into a maze of empty corridors and rooms. Turn to **230**.

233

The scaly green monster's yellow eyes glint with evil intelligence as you unsheathe your sword and take a pace back from the green depths. If you have the skill of Iaijutsu, turn to **357**. Otherwise it produces a strong net from below the surface with which it tries to trap your sword just as you lunge. Roll two dice and add 2 to the score because you may lose your footing on the treacherous slime. If you score less than your SKILL, turn to **171**. If you score equal to or higher than your SKILL, turn to **117**.

234

You put the ancient horn to your lips and blow an ear-shattering blast that echoes across the plain. The tiger stops abruptly. Then it pads slowly towards you, in an attitude of curiosity rather than hunger.

It is as tall as you are, but all it does is lick your face affectionately. You get the impression it thinks you are somebody else, presumably the original owner of the horn. But all that is lost in legend. For now you know it will be waiting to aid you at the Place of Battle. Note this on your *Adventure Sheet*. The tiger looks at you with unnaturally intelligent eyes as you step back through the door to the Hub. Return to **8** and choose again, but not an option you have already tried.

235

Singing Death cuts into Ikiru's side and he hisses with pain. A jagged bolt of lightning leaps from the sword blade and into Ikiru's cowled face. There is an almighty thunderclap, the black runesword disappears and Ikiru is destroyed utterly. No vestige of his being remains in the chamber. Turn to **400**.

236

The bow-shots are accurate and deadly. In the space of a few seconds you have slain the two Shikome, without a sound. You sprint forward and into the palace – there is no time to recover your arrows. Turn to **158**.

237

The journey through the Longhills is easy and within two days you reach the valley of one of the tributaries of the great Hiang-Kiang river. The air is alive with the twittering of song-thrushes as you walk down a rolling green hillside towards the river.

There is a road with white-topped milestones at intervals that runs straight towards the river and you decide to follow it. Turn to **227**.

238

You step forward, draw your sword and hack off the villainous Samurai's head in one fluid motion. 'It is all he deserved for betraying the Shogun and turning to a life of burning and killing,' the headman says. The other villagers thank you for meting out their idea of justice and they give you another gift – six Gold Pieces. After a small celebration you take your leave and head back to the main road. Turn to **24**.

239

The bowel-raker whistles through the air and buries itself in the youth's side. He screams and doubles up in agony then coughs and twitches spasmodically. The wickedly barbed arrow has wounded him badly and he scrabbles at the shaft in an effort to drag the cruel head from his flesh. One of his friends bends to help and the poor youth screams horribly again as the head is jerked free. A torrent of blood flows from the gaping wound. The barbs are designed to prevent easy extraction of the arrow and they have severed vital arteries. The young lad dies in a pool of blood and there are cries of rage from the other charcoal-burners. One drags the moistened turf off one of the mounds, letting out billowing smoke and flames, others seize staves, meaning to do battle. Will you flee (turn to **269**) or fight (turn to **281**)?

240

The arrow whistles past a Samurai's neck. He jumps up in surprise. You try to duck out of sight, but he spots you and cries a warning. Several of the traitorous Samurai turn at his shout and three of them spring towards you. One recognizes you and says, 'The Shogun's – sorry, the *ex*-Shogun's champion. Kill the mangy, flea-ridden goat!' They come at you in a rush, wildly brandishing their swords. You must fight them all at once. If you have the skill of Karumijutsu, you may subtract 1 from all their Attack Rolls for this combat only, as you jump and leap over them, trying to dodge their blows.

	SKILL	STAMINA
First SAMURAI	6	7
Second SAMURAI	8	8
Third SAMURAI	7	6

If you kill all three of them, turn to **154**.

241

Ginsei grins murderously as his katana hisses from its sheath. 'The Shogun's champion. Strange that one so young can be the Shogun's finest sword. It must be that only cowards and babes in arms are so foolish as to pander to that broken reed Hasekawa. I challenge you to single combat, to the death.' He knows that you cannot let such insults pass. You must kill him. He is armed only with his katana. If you have the skill of Iaijutsu and wish to use it, turn to **275**. If you have the skill of Kyujutsu and wish to use it, turn to **289**. Otherwise turn to **301**.

242

The animated skeletons are heaving themselves on to the bridge. If you have the skill of Karumijutsu and wish to sprint forward and attempt to leap over the undead Samurai to the other side of the river, turn to **262**. If not, or you do not wish to try it, the skeletons charge at you. Turn to **358**.

243

You dip the silver ewer into the pool until it is full to the brim and then close the lid. Note it on your *Adventure Sheet*. Taking the chalice, you pour a drop from the ewer and sip it carefully. Knowledge floods your being; for a moment it is as if you were a god, for you have partaken of the Waters of Knowledge. Add 1 to your LUCK for the knowledge of the gods. The Enchanted Garden begins to ripple all around you like a mirage and then it fades away. You find yourself standing on a goat-track at the foot of a mountain, unmistakably one of the Shios'ii range. Ikiru's stronghold lies above, so you begin to ascend. Turn to **8**.

244

One of the arrows buries itself in one of the Shikome's eyes, killing it instantly; the other thwacks into the palace wall. The remaining guard wails in fear and surprise and the alarm goes up. All hell breaks loose and the castle swarms with Samurai and Shikome in seconds. You try to escape, but are soon spotted and are buried under a wave of attackers. Moichi is slain out of hand, but they take you prisoner, making gibes about the Shogun and his champion as they do so – they plainly know who you are. You are filled with sorrow at the loss of your loyal retainer.

You are unceremoniously thrown into a small cell in the palace dungeon. The gaoler, a large beefy man in a stained leather jerkin, says jeeringly, 'You will be taken before the Shogun Tsietsin on the morrow.' He then slams the massive, iron-studded, oaken door of the cell in your face.

You are alone. They have taken your swords, and it is this rather than the cruel gibes and the indignity of capture that fills you with shame. Lose 1 Honour point for their loss. There is nothing you can do but wait for the morning, so you lie down on the wooden pallet in the corner and go to sleep. Turn to **316**.

245
There is no pursuit as you hastily leave the area of the ford, but the Shogun's champion is supposed to keep the roads and river-crossings of the land open and safe for the common folk. You have failed in this duty. Subtract 1 from your Honour and turn to **263**.

246
The great serpent, wide as a tree, tries to bite off your head. You have no choice but to fight it.

GREAT SERPENT   SKILL 10   STAMINA 10

If you win, turn to **272**.

247

The silver Samurai's voice rings out across the Enchanted Garden: 'You are without honour and no Samurai.' You are soon nearing the twin statues of the demon and the captive priestess. The magician appears again out of thin air and the two statues, the black-skinned, red-tusked demon and the pale-skinned priestess come to life. She kneels at your feet imploring you to save her from the Pit of Demons, but her captor yanks the chain cruelly and she is pulled to the floor. The demon throws the chain at your head and speaks the words of the Spell of Petrifaction. You are turned to stone in his place and he is now free. You make a curious counterpoint to the fallen priestess who is now a statue once more. Not until another brave adventurer finds the scarlet pagoda will you taste life again.

248

One of the arrows buries itself in one of the Shikome's eyes, killing it instantly; the other thwacks into the palace wall. The remaining guard wails in fear and surprise and the alarm goes up. All hell breaks loose and the castle swarms with Samurai and Shikome in seconds. You try to escape, but are soon spotted and are buried under a wave of attackers. They take you prisoner, making gibes about the Shogun and his champion as they do so – they plainly know who you are.

You are unceremoniously thrown into a small cell in the palace dungeon. The gaoler, a large beefy man in a stained leather jerkin, says jeeringly, 'You will be taken before the Shogun Tsietsin on the morrow.' He then slams the massive, iron-studded, oaken door of the cell in your face.

You are alone. They have taken your swords and it is this rather than the cruel gibes and the indignity of capture that fills you with shame. Lose 1 Honour point for their loss. There is nothing you can do but wait for the morning, so you lie down on the wooden pallet in the corner and go to sleep. Turn to **316**.

249

The path you have taken into the Spider Fens sinks gradually below the level of the marshes and lakes, high walls of clay holding back the water from the sunken path. You seem to be making good progress. You are nearing the southern edge of the Hiang-Kiang estuary. If you wish to return to the edge of the fen and choose another route, turn back to **17** and choose again. If you wish to continue to the estuary, turn to **33**.

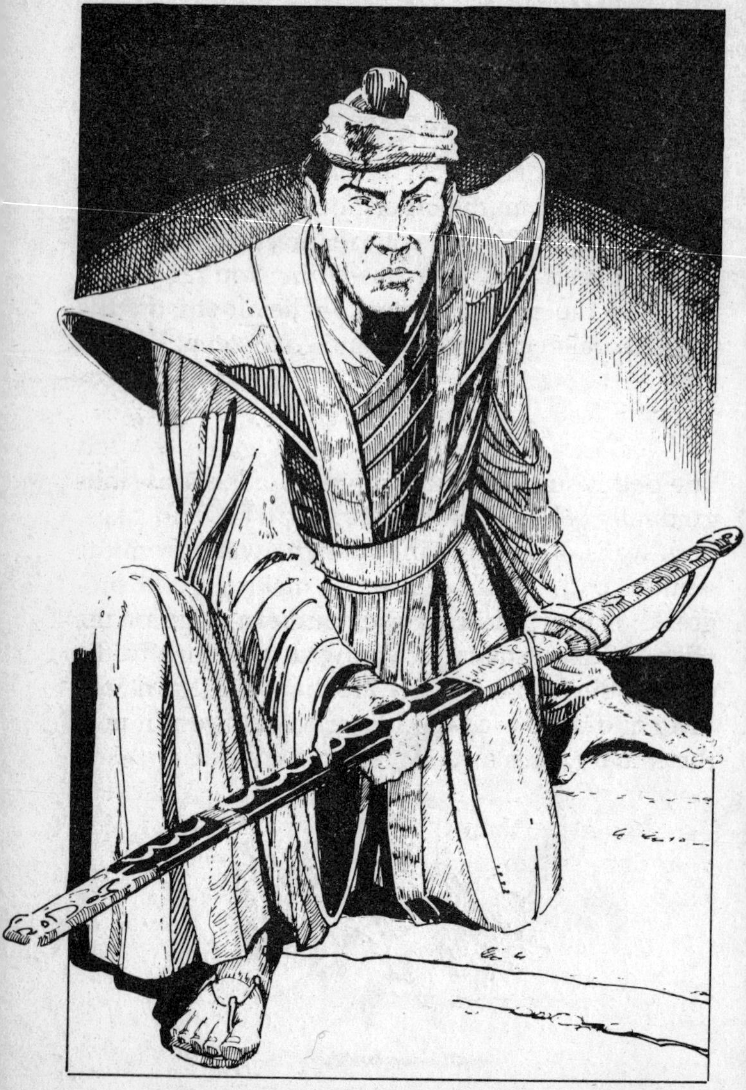

250

'I cannot slay this Samurai in cold blood,' you say loudly, and a cry of disappointment goes up from the villagers. 'But he should pay for his crime!' and 'Revenge, revenge!' they shout.

The captive Samurai sits up in surprise and then bows low before you and offers you his sword. 'Thank you, my lord. My allegiance is to the Shogun Hasekawa still in my heart, but I could not say thus, in the service of Tsietsin as I was. But now I renounce the traitor Tsietsin and pledge my sword to you, my lord. Take me as your loyal companion.' Will you take him with you (turn to **276**), or, if you think he is lying, tell him to return to Tsietsin (turn to **264**)?

251

The brass key is intricately decorated with carvings of serpentine dragons, but there is no clue as to its use. The parchment, however, is a map of the Spider Fens beyond the Hiang-Kiang river. It purports to show a safe route through that forsaken land and there is a path leading to a scarlet seven-tiered pagoda. You stuff key and parchment inside your boot and explore the woods for a dry resting-place. Turn to **371**.

252

You act immediately. You grab your sword and whip it from the scabbard and across the throat of the first Shikome in one fluid motion. It falls, burbling horribly, dead. The other steps back in astonishment and you close in to the attack.

SHIKOME GUARD   SKILL 8   STAMINA 7

If you win, turn to **280**.

253

The old charcoal-burner takes you along a winding track that leads to the vales of Kanshuro, where wooded plateaux are riven by beautiful and peaceful dales which nestle unseen between cliffs cut into the limestone by the rivers which formed them. At dusk you take a path down into the Vale of Tinshu to a small and picturesque village. You turn to the old man to ask its name, but he has fallen to the ground. You try to rouse him, but his heart has stopped. He is dead. Turn to **5**.

254

You will have to face it alone. The toad leaps forward and a mighty battle ensues. You manage to slay Graalsch the toad, and even the mantis, but at the end you are too weak. The Bronze Man comes forward and tears you limb from limb, while the Dai-Oni laughs mockingly. Your adventure ends here.

255

You drop your shoulder and barge into one of the monsters, then knock it off balance with the flat of your sword. A shower of water pours from the hollow basin in the top of its head. It clutches its claws to its head, makes a sound as if it were choking or drowning and dives back into the river. Realizing they use the pool of water on top of their heads to breathe, you concentrate on knocking them off balance so that the water is shed. They are forced to retreat to the river and you are left standing on the bank, tired but victorious. Turn to **393**.

256

You shout an order to Moichi. The Shikome start in surprise and you both fall upon them. You must fight two, while Moichi deals with the other.

	SKILL	STAMINA
First SHIKOME	8	9
Second SHIKOME	7	8

If you have killed them within nine rounds of combat, turn to **336**. Otherwise turn to **218**.

257

The trident's tines bury themselves in your back. If you are wearing armour, turn to **67**. If not, turn to **39**.

258

What will you do? Try to touch the serpent with an antler, if you have one (turn to **290**)? Blow a horn, if you have one (turn to **318**)? Or try to use the Phoenix Ruby in some way, if you have it (turn to **328**)? If you have none of these items, turn to **246**.

259

The Groundhog moves surprisingly quickly on its powerful short legs, but you reach the crest before it and look down upon a breathtaking panorama. The great plain of the lower Hiang-Kiang River lies below you; in the distance is its delta amid the Spider Fens of Kumo. The Spider Fens are lost beneath a pall of mist. Knowing that to detour around the enormous delta would take weeks, you set out down the gentle slope of the valley, leaving the Groundhog behind. Turn to **17**.

260

The cowled figure is unconcerned: he laughs and gestures again. Another formless shape of misty blackness rises from the pit. It forms into a shadowy semblance of yourself, a sight that fills you with fear. But it does not attack you. Instead it reaches into your mind and offers you power, wealth, fame, kingdoms to rule, history to write.

'All these can be yours if you will only swear allegiance to Ikiru, your master,' it whispers in your mind. You feel a terrible compulsion to give in, the temptation is so great; you begin to thirst for power and wealth. If your Honour is 5 or more, turn to **27**. If it is less than 5, turn to **324**.

261

Teeming rain obscures your vision as you climb towards the low hill. The water-level is rising quickly: you might well have drowned if you had not taken this path. As the ground slopes up and you leave the rising waters behind, you notice that all the creatures of the swamp – rats, marsh salamanders and even a giant dragon-newt which seems too scared to contemplate gobbling you up – are racing towards the same patch of high ground to escape the flood. Turn to **149**.

262

You run forward and leap high into the air. *Test your Luck*. If you are Lucky, turn to **286**. If you are Unlucky, turn to **334**.

263

It is not long before new dangers take your mind off those past. Beyond the valley of the upper Hiang-Kiang River lies a ridge of slate that cuts the skyline like a saw. You are nearing the top of this when the whole shelf of slate upon which you are standing begins to tremble. It feels like an earthquake, as if the whole of Hachiman has turned to jelly. There is a low cave near by. You could crawl underneath the overhanging rock (turn to **205**). If you decide instead to lie prone where you are, turn to **103**.

264

You send the man away. The villagers thank you for saving them, but many of them add, 'But I wish you had had the sense to slay that black-hearted, dishonourable Samurai.' After a small celebration, you take your leave and head back to the main road. Turn to **24**.

265

You dash towards the cave, but the Groundhog intercepts you. You must fight it.

GROUNDHOG   SKILL 8   STAMINA 22

If you win, you may enter the cave (turn to **355**).

266

The Mantis Demon K'rllk hurries towards you, its forelegs raised to strike. You must fight the Mantis Demon but, because of its chitinous armour, your blows will only do 1 point of STAMINA damage if you hit it (this can be increased to 2 with a LUCK roll).

MANTIS DEMON   SKILL 8   STAMINA 10

If you win, turn to **346**.

267

As soon as you put down the key, your one good

eye stops its roaming, so you decide to explore the woods for a dry resting-place. You may restore 1 SKILL point. Turn to **371**.

268

You launch desperately into the attack, knowing they are about to do the same. Within seconds you have slain one, but the other begins to howl wildly in fear. In moments the castle is swarming with Samurai and Shikome. You try to escape, but are soon spotted and are buried under a wave of attackers. They take you prisoner, making gibes about the Shogun and his champion as they do so – they plainly know who you are.

You are unceremoniously thrown into a small cell in the palace dungeon. The gaoler, a large beefy man in a stained leather jerkin, says jeeringly, 'You will be taken before the Shogun Tsietsin on the morrow.' He then slams the massive, iron-studded, oaken door of the cell in your face.

You are alone. They have taken your swords, and it is this rather than the cruel gibes and the indignity of capture that fills you with shame. Lose 1 Honour point for their loss. There is nothing you can do but wait for the morning, so you lie down on the wooden pallet in the corner and go to sleep. Turn to **316**.

269

Howls of derision float down the breeze as you hastily put as much distance as you can between yourself and the peasants. It is only when you slow down through lack of breath that the ignominy of having fled when you should have been protecting the honour of the Shogun hits you. If you carry on in this manner you will be utterly without honour and no longer a Samurai. Subtract 2 from your Honour and continue on your way. Turn to **195**.

270

A terrible thing happens. Out of the body of the Dai-Oni, a spectral shape coalesces, a ghostly form of the demon, with insubstantial taloned hands. It is a Shura, or warrior ghost, the spirit of the Dai-Oni come to avenge its death.

You must fight the Shura. When it hits you, you lose STAMINA in the normal way, but there are no wounds; it is draining your strength.

SHURA   SKILL 9   STAMINA 8

If you win, the Shura simply fades away. Turn to **76**.

271

The Legion of the Seventh Seal were the honour guard of the first Shogun. Their like as warriors has never been seen again. They were wiped out when they refused to surrender to a force ten times their size five hundred years ago. The armour is of archaic design but the highest quality. As you prise it free from the rock, the chalcedony flowers break into crystal drops with a tinkling crash, then you are struck a heavy blow from behind. Lose 3 STAMINA points. If you are still alive, you decide to quit the chamber as quickly as possible. Turn to 375.

272

The dead serpent sinks slowly into the mire. Some sleek submerged predator slams into the carcass and begins to consume it as you watch. There is nothing else of interest, so you decide to return to the Hub. Return to 8 and choose again, but you cannot choose an option you have already tried.

273

The ledge is now cracked and has subsided in parts, making the going difficult. At last you come to a smooth area where you decide to eat. As you are reaching into your backpack the ground starts to tremble once more. There is another cave near by. Will you run into it (turn to 329), or lie prone again (turn to 385)?

274

The Shadow Demon lunges at you. You swing

Singing Death in a great two-handed cut. As the sword connects, it gives a single pulse of blazing white light. The Demon howls in agony – a distant faint wail – and its shadowy substance is burst asunder, shards of blackness flying apart until nothing is left. Turn to **212**.

275

Ginsei advances, legs bowed, with the tip of his sword angled towards your throat. You step forward to meet him in single combat, leaving the drawing of your sword so late that he is convinced he has the advantage. Then you draw the blade and strike in one fluid motion, faster than the strike of a cobra. For all your speed, Ginsei too is quick, and he half parries the cut that would have sent his head tumbling from his shoulders, taking the blow instead on his sword-arm. You have wounded him and reduced his SKILL by your sudden strike. Blood runs down over the hilt of his Katana. Now fight on.

GINSEI THE RONIN   SKILL 9   STAMINA 14

If you win, turn to **399**.

276

'Thank you, my lord. You will not regret it,' he says quickly. The villagers begin to disperse, darkly muttering things like 'They're all the same!' As you head back to the main road, he tells you his name is Yomitsume Moichi, and that you can call him Moichi.

You travel north, your Samurai retainer chatting incessantly about his family and his life history, so much so that you begin to regret your decision. At last he falls silent when you round a low hill to see a fortified castle about half a league from the road. 'It is the fortress of Lord Tsietsin the traitor, my lord,' says Moichi quietly. Will you press on with your mission (turn to **288**), or decide that the honour of the Shogun must be upheld and try to enter the castle and slay the traitor (turn to **300**)?

277

You caper up and down, making strange sounds and gestures, but the scaly green monsters are unimpressed. They are forcing you back to the river-bank. Your sword flashes through the air, as a magical barrier of blades surrounded you, but at last one of the creatures gets through your guard. You are knocked to the ground and dragged into the river. You have fallen into the clutches of the Kappa, from which there is no escape.

278

The Ki-Rin takes to the air, its hoofs flashing with fire. As it swoops to the attack, the Mantis Demon waits stock-still. At the last moment, its head lashes forward with blinding speed and bites off the head of the Ki-Rin, whose decapitated body falls out of the sky and then fades out of existence as if it had never been. Remove its name from the list of your allies on your *Adventure Sheet*. The Mantis Demon barely pauses before scuttling towards you. If you are now without allies, turn to **266**. Otherwise which ally will you commit now (use only those listed on your *Adventure Sheet*):

The Tatsu?	Turn to **294**
The Golden Company?	Turn to **304**
The Phoenix?	Turn to **320**
Eleanor the Enchantress?	Turn to **330**

279

The path winds tortuously on and the rain becomes torrential. After a time the water-level begins to rise rapidly until you are knee-deep in water and the route the path takes can only be guessed by tracing lines between the scrawny bulrushes that grow up on either side of it. Will you forge on (turn to **229**), or try to find the route that leads to the low hill you recently passed (turn to **181**)?

280

You step over the bodies of the Shikome guards and into the palace. Turn to **158**.

281

You place your back against a tree, as a cloud of smoke obscures your vision and causes you to cough horribly and your eyes to smart. You force them open as two of the charcoal-burners attack. They have gained the initiative and can attack twice in a row before you can strike back. Your first two Attack Rolls count only as attempts to parry: you do not inflict any loss of STAMINA if you win.

	SKILL	STAMINA
First CHARCOAL-BURNER	6	10
Second CHARCOAL-BURNER	7	9

If you kill the first of your attackers without being hurt yourself, turn to **347**. If you have been wounded by their staves by the time you have killed one of them, turn to **365**.

282

He opens the door and walks towards where you lie huddled on the pallet. He leans over you. Suddenly you twist around and drive your fist at him. He reels back in surprise. You must fight the gaoler, but deduct 2 from your SKILL as you do not have your swords.

GAOLER   SKILL 7   STAMINA 7

If you kill the gaoler in four combat rounds or less, turn to **308**. If it takes five or more rounds, turn to **332**.

283

Your feet slide across the slime and you are on the brink of disaster when one of your feet catches against the shell of a giant water-snail and you regain your balance so that you can teeter to the far bank, just as another of the scaly green monsters rises from the depths. Turn to **297**.

284

You gather your legs beneath you and leap high into the air, the years of training in this art enabling you to achieve heights many think impossible. It is just enough for you to catch at the battlements and, like a shade, you slide over the wall into the castle. Quickly you hide behind a stable.

Across the castle courtyard is a square stone keep, with pagoda-like roofs and carved gables, the palace of Lord Tsietsin. But it is the two palace guards flanking the doors that really draw your attention. They are Shikome, vile humanoid beings, but hairy as apes, and with claws, fangs and horrible snouted faces. They are dressed in dirty and tattered imitations of Samurai armour, although their weapons seem in excellent condition. The presence of Shikome can only mean that Tsietsin is in league with Ikiru, Master of Shadows. Tsietsin will be in the palace, and it seems even more important than before to slay him.

When it is late evening, you decide to act. If you have the skill of Kyujutsu, you can try to kill both the guards as swiftly as possible with two single bow-shots (turn to **46**). If you cannot, or do not wish to use this skill, you can walk casually towards them and then suddenly attack (turn to **64**), walk forward and say you have an important message for Lord Tsietsin (turn to **84**) or simply stride forward as authoritatively as possible, salute and walk into the palace as if they were not there (turn to **100**).

285

The track you have taken winds tortuously through the mire until you have lost all sense of direction. If you wish to return to the edges of the fen and choose another route, go back to **17**. If instead you forge ahead, turn to **309**.

286

You fly over the undead warrior and land nimbly on the other side. The sky is suddenly lighter. Turning around you see to your surprise that the Samurai is no longer there, nor are the skeletal warriors. The river flows cleanly and is untainted. Leaves swirl about the bridge in a soft breeze. You decide not to linger, so you continue on the road. Turn to **211**.

287

You cannon in your blindness into the doorpost, but the feel of soft turf underfoot and the wind on your cheek confirm that you have made it out of the hovel. After a few minutes, during which you do no more than risk a dozen faltering steps, one of your eyes pops back into place. You can see again, but with only one eye you cannot co-ordinate your sword-strokes, and at times your good eye rolls around at random making you virtually blind again. Subtract 2 from your SKILL. If you wish to leave the key and the parchment which brought such bad luck, turn to **267**. If you scrutinize them as best you can, turn to **251**.

288

You continue on your way, and Moichi's mood lightens. He keeps talking and, although irritating, he seems a simple fellow who honourably follows the Way of Bushido closely. Presently the road curves between two steep, wooded hills, and you and Moichi walk on through the pleasant valley. *Test your Luck*. If you are Lucky, turn to **106**. If you are not, turn to **120**.

289

As Ginsei advances, legs bowed, his sword-tip angled towards your throat, you notch an arrow to your bow and let fly. Ginsei's blade is a blur of motion as he cuts the arrow in two, knocking the head aside just before it pierces him. He sneers malevolently. 'So you fight like an ashigaru, a peasant soldier. I care nothing for your underhand tricks.' You have used your bow against a man armed only with a sword who has challenged you to single combat. You are dishonoured by your unfair action. Subtract 1 from your Honour. Turn to **301**.

290

The serpent's head arcs down towards you, but you dodge aside and rap it smartly with the antler. The effect is startling. A pulse of magical energy flows through you. The serpent and the antler abruptly disappear in a flash of blue light. In their place lies a thin rod of dark wood. Around it writhes a stylized serpent, carved into the wood. You pick it up – power flows through it – and pocket it. Note it on your *Adventure Sheet*. You turn and step through the door, back to the Hub. Return to **8** and choose again, but you cannot choose an option you have tried already.

291

Your sword has been making no impression on the steely silver skin of the Samurai. Your brow drips with sweat. If you wish to flee and try to take the path which leads to the statues of the priestess and the demon, turn to **247**. If you refuse to let your honour be tarnished through flight, turn to **81**.

292

You must fight the Dai-Oni. Whenever it hits you, you lose 2 STAMINA points as in normal combat, but also roll one extra die: if the result is 1 or 2, turn to **90**; if the result is 3 or 4, turn to **102**; if the result is 5 or 6, turn to **118**.

DAI-ONI   SKILL 10   STAMINA 10

If you win, turn to **74**.

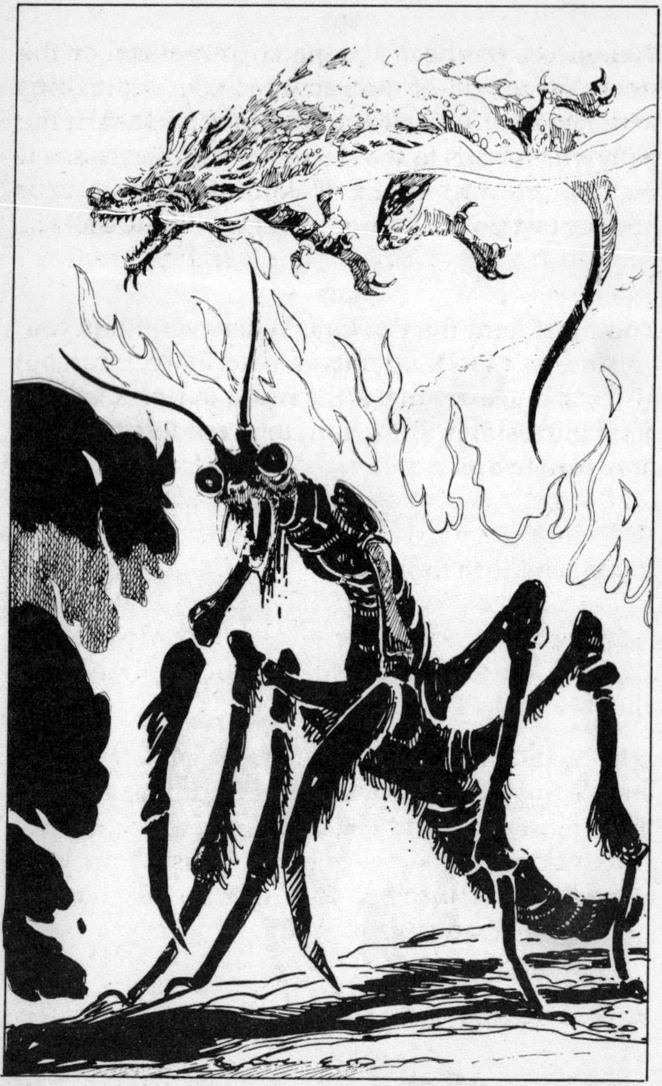

293

As you stride forward menacingly, several of the peasants break and flee deep into the woods. Seeing that they have been deserted by their comrades, the others throw down their staves and follow suit. If you feel that you have done enough to protect the good name of your lord, you may continue on your way (turn to **195**). If you are determined to teach them a lesson, turn to **331**.

294

The Tatsu gallops into the air and dives straight at K'rllk. Just as the Mantis Demon rears back to strike, the Tatsu breathes a stream of flame from its mouth that engulfs the Mantis Demon, which burns like straw and is reduced to ashes within seconds. The Tatsu turns to you, 'Farewell, manling, and good fortune: I must leave you now.' With that it rides away into the skies. The ghostly crowd seems to applaud as if from a great distance. The Dai-Oni is almost apoplectic with rage.

'Kill, Gargantus, kill!' he screams, and the huge bronze goat-man lumbers forward. If you are now without allies, turn to **364**. Otherwise which ally will you commit now (use only those listed on your *Adventure Sheet*): the Ki-Rin (turn to **382**), or the Golden Company (turn to **198**)?

295

As you reach the crest, a vast panorama opens up. The great valley of the lower Hiang-Kiang River lies below you. In the distance lies its delta amid the Spider Fens of Kumo. The Spider Fens are lost in a pall of mist. Knowing that to detour around the enormous delta would take weeks, you set off down the gentle slope of the valley. Turn to **17**.

296

He ignores your moans of pain and moves on, waking other prisoners, sliding black bread and stale water through flaps in the doors. Presently he returns and opens your cell door. But this time he has three soldiers with him. Will you pretend to have been wounded and then suddenly attack them (turn to **370**), or pretend to have been wounded and, when they have taken you out of the cell, grab a weapon and try to run away (turn to **380**)?

297

You take up a defensive position near the far bank of the river, as several more of the scaly green monsters rise dripping from the depths and converge on you. If you have the skill of Karumijutsu and wish to try to leap over their heads to safety, turn to **35**. If you decide to stand your ground and fight it out, turn to **13**. If instead you surrender, turn to **3**.

298

You skirt the pit and walk towards the throne, holding Singing Death in front of you. As you near it, the shadows fall back, unable to resist the power of the sword. Those that stray too close are instantly vaporized by its touch. Turn to **121**.

299

Inside, the scarlet pagoda is clean but bare, except for a mirror in a screen before you. You reach forward to touch it and it seems to absorb first your hand and then the whole of you. Before you know what is happening you are standing in the most beautiful garden you have ever seen. At its centre is an ornamental pond into which bubbles a crystal clear spring. Several winding paths lead from the point where you stand to the pond but the most interesting thing about the garden apart from the flowers and climbers, which are a riot of colour, are the statues.

There are five magnificent statues in all. The nearest one on the left is of a silver Samurai; the nearest on the right comprises a young priestess kneeling down with a terrible demon behind her, who holds a chain that is fastened around her neck. She is marked with a dragonfly tattoo on her bared shoulder. Separate paths lead to these statues and, beyond them, are two still more fearsome stone colossi. One is of Hammurabi, the Lord of Flies, in the form of a gigantic dragonfly. The other is of the dreaded Sea Dragon, which rises from its pedestal like a waterspout. Turn to **137**.

300

Gain 1 Honour point for your brave decision. Moichi's face falls when you tell him, but then he says, 'Well, my lord, I suppose that is the honourable thing to do. I know a hidden postern gate at the rear of the castle and the password – we can gain entrance there with ease, if you will allow this humble warrior to lead such a one as you, O mighty lord.' He bows low. You cannot quite tell whether or not Moichi is being sarcastic in his praise of you, but you tell him to lead on anyway. He smiles roughly and leads you by a roundabout route to the rear of the castle where it nestles against the foothills of the southern Shios'ii Mountains. You wait until nightfall before approaching the hidden gate. Moichi walks up to a section of the wall and knocks on it. A slat opens and two eyes, glittering in the moonlight, stare out. 'Who goes there?' a voice hisses. 'It is I, Moichi. We have returned from a night patrol on Lord Tsietsin's personal orders. The password is "Cherry Blossom".' With that, the door slides open, allowing you and Moichi to step in. Without a word, you drive your fist into the surprised guard's face. The guard falls without a sound. Turn to **136**.

301

Ginsei advances, legs bowed, with the tip of his sword angled towards your throat. You meet him in single combat.

GINSEI THE RONIN   SKILL 10   STAMINA 16

If you win, turn to **399**.

302

You must fight them both.

	SKILL	STAMINA
First SAMURAI	7	9
Second SAMURAI	8	7

If you kill them both, turn to **310**.

303

Both of your eyes roll up into your head, making you completely blind; then one rolls back into place and you can make out a large brass key beneath the puppet and some creased and greasy parchment. Taking both key and parchment, you throw the box outside and feel your way to the door of the hovel as your eyes roll up into your head once more. Turn to **287**.

304

The knights of the Golden Company utter a battle-cry and charge forward with military precision. However, their weapons, straight swords and maces, make little impression on the chitinous armour of the Mantis Demon. K'rllk lays about itself with ferocious accuracy, each super-fast dart of its head biting a knight in two. Within moments they are all dead. You stand aghast at its horrible power. Remove the knights from the list of allies on your *Adventure Sheet*. K'rllk turns upon you and scuttles forward. If you are now without allies, turn to **266**. Otherwise which ally will you commit now (use only those listed on your *Adventure Sheet*): the Tatsu (turn to **294**) or the Ki-Rin (turn to **278**)?

305

You have slain the Groundhog. You try on the armour: it is a good fit, and you may add 1 to your SKILL while wearing it. There is nothing else here, so you climb to the crest to see what lies beyond. Turn to **295**.

306

A troop of fifteen riders appears on the road ahead of you. They are wearing blue and green lacquered battle armour and you recognize the symbol emblazoned on a banner one of them bears. They are Samurai of Lord Tsietsin. At the sight of you, they spur their horses into a charge, one of them shouting, 'It's the Shogun's lackey – take him!' There is nowhere to run to and soon they are upon you. You struggle mightily, slaying three of them and wounding several more, but there are too many and soon you are securely bound and strapped over a horse's back. 'Lord Tsietsin will be pleased with this little catch,' one of them quips.

They take you to the castle you passed on the road. You are led into the courtyard, where many of Lord Tsietsin's Samurai retainers gather around to laugh and mock you. You are unceremoniously thrown into a small cell in the palace dungeon. The gaoler, a large beefy man in a stained leather jerkin, says jeeringly, 'You will be taken before the Shogun Tsietsin on the morrow.' He then slams the massive, iron-studded, oaken door of the cell in your face.

You are alone. They have taken your swords, and it is this rather than the cruel gibes and the indignity of capture that fills you with shame. Lose 1 Honour point for their loss. There is nothing you can do but wait for the morning, so you lie down on the wooden pallet in the corner and go to sleep. Turn to **316**.

307

The bravest of the charcoal-burners, four tough-looking weather-beaten men, charge you together, brandishing their staves. You must fight them, but you wisely back up against a tree, so that only two can assail you at once.

	SKILL	STAMINA
First CHARCOAL-BURNER	6	10
Second CHARCOAL-BURNER	7	9

If you kill the first of your attackers without being hurt, turn to **347**. If you have been wounded by the time you have killed one of them, turn to **365**.

308

Your last blow lays out the gaoler. Without hesitating, you run out of the cell. You are in a long, cell-lined, torch-lit corridor that stretches into darkness to left and right. Will you turn left (turn to **344**) or right (turn to **356**)?

309

After another half a day, during which you make slow but steady progress, only occasionally stepping off the path into the mire, it begins to rain. The mist thins until a low hill in the middle of the fens is revealed a few miles to the east. A small path diverges from the path you are on towards it. Will you take the path that leads to the hill (turn to **261**), or press on (turn to **279**)?

310

Sheathing your blade, you spring after Lord Tsietsin. Soon you have caught up with him, just in time to see him ducking through a black and gold lacquered door. You follow, and burst into a large, richly decorated room, with a black and gold lacquered chest in one corner. Tsietsin, gibbering in fear, has raised a trap-door in one corner of the room. When he sees that you will reach him before he can manoeuvre his vast bulk down it, he falls to his knees before you. Turn to **178**.

311

You clamber on to a mossy mound near the far bank of the river as several more of the scaly green monsters rise dripping from the depths and converge on you. If you have the skill of Karumijutsu and wish to try to leap over their heads to safety, turn to **35**. If you decide to stand your ground and fight it out, turn to **13**. If instead you surrender, turn to **3**.

312

You walk forward and cast the sword into the pit. Ikiru leaps up and cries, 'No, don't.' His voice is like the rustle of leaves. As the sword disappears from sight, the hall begins to shudder. The shadows around Ikiru begin to shred and break up. His throne begins to crumble and a keening wind rushes through the hall. It strikes Ikiru and begins to rip him apart. He is scattered like chaff and destroyed. Everything begins to crumble about you and the pit falls in on itself, burying Singing Death. You manage to escape the destruction and although you have slain Ikiru, Singing Death is forever lost in the nether regions.

When you return to Konichi, the Shogun thanks you, but sinks into a grim depression. Without Singing Death, Hachiman begins to collapse as a state. Rebel lords break away and barbarian raids soon become full-blown invasions, often allied to local rebel lords. It is in one of these campaigns that you are slain, trying to defend your nation. But it is all to no avail: Hachiman sinks into a new dark age, and ultimately you have failed.

313

Your feverish tearing loosens the fastenings of each piece of armour one by one, and they drift into the depths. At last you break the surface and throw your swords to the edge of the pool before climbing out. Luckily the well-shaft opens out on to a natural water-filled cave and there is a ledge just above the water-level. By feeling around in the darkness you locate a tunnel which you decide to explore. Your armour is lost in the depths of the pool: until you find another suit to fit you, all weapons will do 4 STAMINA points of damage every time you are hit in combat, instead of just 2. Turn to **363**.

314

Will you press on down the road and try to skirt past Tsietsin's home without being spotted (turn to **338**), or decide that the honour of the Shogun must be upheld and try to get into the castle and slay Lord Tsietsin (turn to **350**)?

315

If you have the skill of Kyujutsu and wish to try to scare them off with a humming-bulb arrow, turn to **21**. Otherwise you try a swing with your sword as the nearest of the monsters attacks. Turn to **53**.

316

Thin arrows of sunlight penetrate your dark cell from the small window the next day. You awake to the sound of a rattle at your cell door. It is the gaoler. 'Wake up, you dog,' he cries. 'I shall be coming to take you to Tsietsin soon!' He is about to move on. Will you moan loudly as if you were very ill or badly wounded, hoping he will come in so that you can attack him (turn to **20**), or wait until he returns (turn to **40**)?

317

The dyke runs for mile after mile, the product of an ancient civilization that lived in the delta before the eternal mists descended. After a while the map directs you to take a path that leads down to the shore of the lake, where it forks. One fork leads to a crescent of basalt stepping-stones, great hexagonal columns of rock, a veritable giant's causeway that leads deep into the mist. The other leads into a peat bog which is labelled on the map with a skull transfixed by a sword. Will you brave the giant's causeway (turn to **113**), or the bog (turn to **217**)? The map suggests that the pagoda lies at the end of one of these, but it is not plain which.

318

The horn gives an ear-splitting blast, which echoes through the miasmal swamp, but it is as if the serpent has no ears at all. Turn to **246**.

319

A circle of ten of the most venerable-looking peasants surround the well outside the headman's house. They part deferentially to allow you within their circle, and the headman, who carries a ribbon of office and the headman's medal, invites you to stay with them until their business is finished. Then, surprisingly, they ignore you and go on talking about village matters. Indeed, strangely enough, they seem to be deciding whether or not to stop planting crops altogether. The western sky is a blaze of sunset red. Will you leave the village and walk off into the sunset (turn to **11**), or wait for them to finish (turn to **155**)?

320

The Phoenix takes to the air and hurtles towards the Mantis Demon. At the last moment it halts, hovering before K'rllk's threshing jaws. Just as the Mantis Demon rears back to strike, the Phoenix engulfs

320

itself in golden flame. The Mantis cannot stop itself thrusting forward into the fire – and is instantly consumed. Within seconds it is nothing but ash. The Phoenix gives a cry of triumph and then soars skyward and away. Remove its name from the list of your allies. The Dai-Oni is almost apoplectic with rage.

'Kill, Gargantus, kill!' he screams and the huge bronze goat-man lumbers forward. If you are now without allies, turn to **364**. Otherwise which ally will you commit now (use only those listed on your *Adventure Sheet*): the Ki-Rin (turn to **382**) or Eleanor the Enchantress (turn to **22**)?

321

You decline to meet the silver Samurai in single combat. 'Then you are a man without honour, lower than a beast which was born without honour and cannot be dishonoured. You deserve only dishonourable death.' You have refused the time-honoured challenge of a Samurai to fight in the name of your lord the Shogun. Subtract 2 from your Honour. The silver Samurai steps forward to do battle; the sun flashing off his skin almost dazzles you.

SILVER SAMURAI   SKILL 10   STAMINA 12

If you hit him three times, turn to **291**.

322

The traitor, Lord Tsietsin, is dead. The honour of the Shogun and of Hachiman has been upheld. Gain 1 Honour point for ridding the land of the evil Lord Tsietsin, and for killing him in the middle of his own castle. You look around the room. Mostly it is full of ornate decoration, but the large chest catches your interest. You quickly open it. Inside is a bag of 100 Gold Pieces, an arrow and an excellently crafted suit of Samurai armour, obviously too small for the overweight Tsietsin. You don the armour, and find it is far superior to your own, especially because it is made out of some unusually light metal. Gain 1 SKILL point.

If you have the skill of Kyujutsu, you recognize the arrow as being crafted by the legendary master of

Kyujutsu, Tsunewara, who is reputed to have had magical powers. It is fletched with white eagle feathers. It should have the power of dispelling evil spirits. Note it on your *Adventure Sheet*.

Sudden sounds of shouting and the clash of weapons come from outside. Tsietsin's men will be here any minute. You dart down the open trap-door and close it behind you. Stairs lead down into stygian blackness. You carefully descend: turn to **122**.

323

You land on the edge of the pier of rock and then helplessly roll into the frothing white waters below. Unfortunately the scaly green monsters have placed sharpened spikes just below the surface upon which you are now impaled. Your armour is pierced in several places and you lose 5 STAMINA points. If you are still alive, you manage to drag yourself off the spikes and are washed up on the far bank just out of the clutches of two of the monsters. Turn to **311**.

324

You succumb to its lure. 'Power and wealth will be mine,' you think to yourself and you fall on one knee and offer your sword to Ikiru, saying, 'I am your loyal slave, O master.' The demon he summoned vanishes and Ikiru laughs – a sound like the rustling of leaves. 'You fool,' he whispers and orders you to kill yourself. You find that you cannot resist his will and gash open your stomach, to die in agony.

325

Before you can say a word, one of the Kappa throws a trident from beneath the waters. *Test your Luck*. If you are Lucky, turn to **367**. If you are Unlucky, turn to **373**.

326

Will you carry on down the road (turn to **362**), or pay a visit to Lord Tsietsin and ask him to help you in some way (turn to **376**)?

327

The chest splinters as it hits the floor and a small metal object spins across the floor, but you are outside the hovel in a twinkling and decide to search the woods for a dry resting-place. Your eyes stop rolling around in your head quite soon, but one of them wanders about from time to time, as if you had a bad squint. Sometimes it rolls up into your head so that you can't see through it at all. Your swordplay will suffer until the puppet dragon's curse is lifted. Subtract 1 from your SKILL, then turn to **371**.

328
You hold up the ruby in front of it, but it takes no notice and remains intent on making you its next meal. Turn to **246**.

329
As soon as you reach the cave the trembling stops, but you decide to enter in case it had presaged a more violent quake. You light a torch and see that the cave is in fact a small grotto filled with pink chalcedony flowers, like a bed of coral. Lying on top of the rock flowers is a magnificent suit of lacquered armour, a little dusty and mouldy but still resplendent in the gold and blue colours of the Legion of the Seventh Seal. Will you take the armour (turn to **271**), or leave straight away (turn to **375**)?

330
Eleanor rushes forward. The Mantis Demon towers above her, but she puts her hands together and unleashes a ravening bolt of blue energy. However, incredibly, it coruscates against the Mantis's chitinous armour and is deflected to fade into the air. The Mantis whips its head forward, bites into her and gobbles her up horribly. Remove Eleanor's name from the list of allies on your *Adventure Sheet*.

K'rllk hardly hesitates; it scuttles towards you. If you are now without allies, turn to **266**. Otherwise which ally will you commit now (use only those listed on your *Adventure Sheet*): the Phoenix (turn to **320**) or the Ki-Rin (turn to **278**)?

331

Brandishing your katana, you plunge into the wood on the trail of the impudent youth. He breaks cover and sprints across a clearing in full view, but as you turn to follow a trap closes on your shin, splintering your greaves and holding you fast in a vice-like grip. You fall heavily and stifle a groan. The trap is made of iron: you might die of thirst before managing to extricate yourself. Subtract 3 from your STAMINA score. If you are still alive, will you cry out to the charcoal-burners for help (turn to **37**) or lie low and wait (turn to **65**)?

332

The sound of battle brings more guards and they dash into the cell. One of them spears you in the chest and the blood bubbles up into your lungs. You slump to the dirty floor of the cell, to drown in your own blood.

333

The trident's tines have pierced your armour and broken one of your ribs. Lose 2 STAMINA points. If you are still alive and wish to leave immediately, turn to **335**. If you drag the trident out of your flesh and use it to threaten the Kappa, while trying to talk to them, turn to **361**.

334

Your leap did not take you high enough. The undead Samurai manages to catch your legs and bring you tumbling to the ground. You spring to your feet, but the skeletons surround you now. Turn to **358**.

335

There is no pursuit as you leave the Kappa's ford and it is not long before new dangers take your mind off those past. Beyond the valley of the upper Hiang-Kiang lies a ridge of slate that cuts the skyline like a saw. You are nearing the top of this when the whole shelf of slate upon which you are standing begins to tremble. It feels like an earthquake, as if the whole of Hachiman has turned to jelly. There is a low cave near by: you could crawl underneath the overhanging rock (turn to **205**). If you decide instead to lie prone where you are, turn to **103**.

336

Moichi is wounded, but has killed his opponent. You pause for breath and Moichi grins at you happily. 'Well fought, my lord. It is an honour to fight by your side.' He bows obsequiously. 'Enough of this veiled mockery,' you reply. 'On to the heart of the palace!'

You run down a long corridor and soon find yourself lost in a maze of corridors and rooms, mostly empty save for servants and slaves, who stare at you in amazement. You are rounding a corner when you are greeted by a sight that causes you to pull up short in surprise. You have bumped into Lord Tsietsin himself, waddling down the corridor towards you, a Samurai at either side. Lord Tsietsin is a large fat man with great blubbery jaws and a face wreathed in fat. Two pig-like eyes flare at you in outrage. He wears a voluminous kimono, adorned with gold leaf. You notice that he is quite openly wearing the hat which indicates the office of Shogun.

Tsietsin gasps in fear as he recognizes you, signals to his guards, turns around and lumbers away from you. The Samurai draw their blades, bow and dash to the attack. Moichi darts forward and engages one. You must fight the other.

TSIETSIN'S
  BODYGUARD   SKILL 9   STAMINA 8

If you win, turn to 354.

337

The Groundhog is like a walking platform with a broad back and eight stumpy legs. In the middle of its back a huge slit-like mouth has opened up and the edges, which have turned upwards to all but envelop you, have a line of tails with hard balls of bone at the ends, like living morning stars. You draw your katana to give battle, but it will not be easy, balanced precariously on the Groundhog's back as you are. Subtract 1 from your SKILL score for this battle only.

GROUNDHOG   SKILL 8   STAMINA 22

If you win, you go on to investigate the cave. Turn to **355**.

338
You trudge on. The land is less cultivated here, wilder and more overgrown. Soon you are travelling between two wooded hills through a shallow valley. *Test your Luck*. If you are Lucky, turn to **386**. If you are Unlucky, turn to **306**.

339
The winding path crosses many more and eventually has you completely lost in the mist. You pause to try to and get your bearings; then it begins to rain, even though it is still misty. It rains hard for two whole days until the water-level has risen above your head. There is no escape from the Spider Fens. You swim many miles, but die exhausted.

340

The Ki-Rin gazes at you benevolently, filling you with peace and tranquillity. 'Your cause is a just one, mortal, and you are a worthy choice for its completion. You are of good heart. Because of this, I shall aid you. I will be at the Place of Battle, to fight with you against the Dai-Oni and his evil allies.' Its voice is lovely to listen to. You are about to thank it when it utters a wild cry and takes to the air, leaving you alone. A door appears, hanging in the air before you. You step through it and find yourself back in the Hub, surrounded by stars and the eight doors. Make a note on your *Adventure Sheet* that the Ki-Rin is your ally. Return to **8** and choose again, but you cannot choose an option that you have already tried.

341

The silver Samurai steps forward to do battle. The sun flashing on his skin almost dazzles you.

SILVER SAMURAI   SKILL 10   STAMINA 12

If you hit him three times, turn to **291**.

342

You are away before the guards have reacted, but when they see where you are going they do not chase after you. Soon you come to a room filled with weapons, clothes and the like. In it you find your swords, but also that there is no way out. You are trapped. You dash back up the corridor, but already there are more than ten guards waiting for you.

They charge forward. You fight valiantly, slaying several in the close confines of the corridor, but at last a spear thrust spills your guts on to the dungeon floor and ends your life.

343
The flimsy material weighs next to nothing and you stuff it into your pack before leaving the hut and searching the woods for a dry resting-place. Turn to **371**.

344
You run left, past dank and stinking prison walls. There is a shout from up ahead – 'Hida, is that you?' – and then a muffled curse and the sound of running feet: a guard is coming towards you. You try to hide in the shadow of the corridor, but it is too light. However, the sight of you takes him completely by surprise, which allows you to strike him hard. He staggers back, but draws his sword and comes back at you, his face a mask of rage and pain. You must fight him, but subtract 2 from your SKILL as you have no swords.

GUARD   SKILL 7   STAMINA 9

If you win, turn to **88**.

345

Eyes smarting from the stinging gas which the Forsaken One gives out when its flesh is pierced, you struggle on down the tunnel and, mercifully, into the open air low on a hillside near the village. It seems the Rokuro-Kubi have stopped at the undead corpse of the Forsaken One and you can escape their village. Add 1 to your LUCK for surviving them, and turn to **397**.

346

The Mantis Demon lies dead before you, oozing black ichor. The Dai-Oni angrily shouts, 'Gargantus, slay the mortal!' And the Bronze Man lumbers towards you. Turn to **364**.

347

You seem impervious to their blows, and when you have slain one the others prostrate themselves at your feet, begging for mercy. You tell them that they are fools to think they could harm the Shogun's champion. The oldest tells you that if you spare him he can show you to a village where you may pass the night safely. Will you tell him to lead on (turn to **179**), or demand that they swear an oath of allegiance to the Shogun (turn to **163**)?

348

As the Phoenix draws near, you feel a strange burning in your backpack. You reach in and pull out the Phoenix Ruby. It is growing hot and radiating a deep glow that bathes you in reddish light. Instinc-

348

tively, you hold it up. The Phoenix utters another wild cry and golden flames burst from it, so that it becomes a fireball for a brief instant. Then it lands a little way from you, regarding you strangely, membranes flicking across the ruby glow of its eyes from time to time. It imparts a message to you without speaking:

'I shall aid you. Look for me at the Place of Battle, O bearer of the Ruby.' Then it flies away. Note that the Phoenix is your ally. You turn and step through the door. Return to **8** and choose another option, but you cannot choose one you have chosen already.

349

You are nearing the twin statues of the demon and the captive priestess. The magician appears again out of thin air and the two statues, the black-skinned, red-tusked demon and the pale-skinned priestess come to life. She kneels at your feet imploring you to save her from the Pit of Demons, but her captor yanks the chain cruelly and she is pulled to the floor. The demon throws the chain at your head and speaks the words of the Spell of Petrifaction. You are turned to stone in its place and it is now free. You make a curious counterpoint to the fallen priestess who is now a statue once more. Not until another brave adventurer finds the scarlet pagoda will you taste life again.

350

Gain 1 Honour point for your brave decision. You head purposefully towards Lord Tsietsin's castle. As you near it, you can pick out the soldiers lining the walls from the glint of their weapons in the sunlight. Will you walk boldly up to the entrance and try to bluff your way in (turn to **374**), or skirt the walls and try to find a place where you could scale them (turn to **388**)?

351

Your arrow misses, but the charcoal-burners have taken the hint. They melt away into the woods from which they cut the materials of their trade. Only the oldest of them stays behind with his son, saying that he will show you to a safe place to spend the night so that it may not be said that his family have dishonoured a Samurai. Turn to **179**.

352

The Ki-Rin eyes you distastefully. It gives you a withering look of contempt and scorn before taking to the air, leaving you alone on the mountain peak, where an icy wind blows up and sheets of rain begin to drench you. A door appears in the air in front of you and you seize your opportunity to escape the elements by stepping through it. You find yourself back at the Hub, surrounded by stars and the eight doors. Return to **8** and choose again, but you cannot choose an option you have already tried.

353

Your hands scrabble feverishly at the fastenings of your armour, but the chill waters sap your strength and lack of oxygen causes you to pass out suddenly. By the time the Rokuro-Kubi start to dine on your tender flesh you are long drowned.

354

Moichi has also killed his opponent, but is slightly wounded. Sheathing your blade, you spring after Lord Tsietsin. Soon you have caught up with him, just in time to see him ducking through a black and gold lacquered door. You and Moichi follow and burst into a large richly decorated room, with a black and gold lacquered chest in one corner. Tsietsin, gibbering in fear, has raised a trap-door in one corner of the room. When he sees that you will reach him before he can manoeuvre his vast bulk down it, he falls to his knees before you.

'Spare me, great warrior, please spare me. It was Ikiru: he forced me to turn against the rightful Shogun, forgive me, I shall be his loyal vassal from now on,' he gabbles, a tissue of transparent lies. As you look down, feeling only contempt and loathing, Tsietsin's eyes narrow in cunning malice. His right hand flicks through the air. A needle-like dagger flies from his hand and into your thigh. Lose 3 STAMINA points. If you are still alive, you stagger back in surprise, as he lurches to his feet, drawing his sword. 'Curse you, you swine,' he cries and slashes at you.

Moichi leaps forward and within moments, both of you have ended Tsietsin's miserable life. Turn to **366**.

355

By the light of a torch you see that the cave is in fact a small grotto filled with pink chalcedony flowers, like a bed of coral. Lying on top of the rock flowers is a magnificent suit of lacquered armour, a little dusty, but still resplendent in the gold and blue colours of the Legion of the Seventh Seal. The

355

Legion of the Seventh Seal were the honour guard of the first Shogun. Their like as warriors has never been seen since. They were wiped out when they refused to surrender to a force ten times their size five hundred years ago. The armour is of archaic design but the highest quality. There is a tinkling crash as you shatter some of the flowers in dislodging the armour, but you are pleased to see that it fits and is miraculously light. You may add 1 to your SKILL while wearing this armour, thanks to the magic it contains. There is little else in the grotto, so you leave and climb to the crest to see what lies beyond. Turn to **295**.

356

You run right, past cell doors. The corridor opens out into a large square room – a complete dead end. However, it is lined with weapons, clothes, and other bits and pieces. To your joy, stacked in a corner are all your weapons. Quickly you pick them up and you feel whole once more. Gain 1 LUCK point for reclaiming your swords. There is a good selection of arrows here: if you are a master of Kyujutsu, you may replenish any arrows you have lost, up to twelve, or reorganize the types of your arrows as you wish.

There is nothing else of interest to you, so you turn round and run back down the corridor and past your old cell. Turn to **132**.

357

A split second after your hand falls upon the hilt of your katana, the head of the nearest monster is sailing end over end towards the far bank. Its headless torso, still gripping a net, sinks lifeless beneath the surface. The second monster is still surging towards the ford, and you just have time to reach the far bank, teetering dangerously on the green slime every step of the way. Turn to **395**.

358

There are six skeletons animated by the undead Samurai, but only three of them can get at you at a time. You must fight them all at once.

	SKILL	STAMINA
First SKELETON	6	7
Second SKELETON	7	6
Third SKELETON	7	7

If you defeat them all, you must fight the next three.

	SKILL	STAMINA
Fourth SKELETON	7	6
Fifth SKELETON	6	7
Sixth SKELETON	8	9

If you defeat these three, turn to **368**.

359

You gingerly remove the chest from the secret cupboard and set it on the straw-covered floor. Then, using the tip of your wakizashi, you prise open the clasp, while shielding your eyes against any possible spray of flame. The clasp breaks and the lid flies open to reveal a puppet dragon, like a jack-in-the-box. Two clouds of steam jet out from the puppet's nostrils and bathe your head in orange smoke. It seems to seep into your eyes, which itch and start to roll around in your head of their own accord. Will you throw down the chest and leave (turn to **327**), or sneak a look at what lies beneath the puppet (turn to **303**)?

360

The Phoenix swoops dangerously close to you. Suddenly it bursts into flame, becoming for an instant a golden fireball, and you are singed by its flames. Lose 2 STAMINA points. If you still live, will you fight the Phoenix (turn to **372**), or try to run back through the door hanging behind you (turn to **390**)?

361

You decide to threaten that you will bring an army of Samurai to kill the Kappa unless they can help in your quest. The yellow eyes bob up and down in the gloom, then one rises suddenly to the surface and throws a sparkling red gem at your feet. 'It is our greatest treasure,' it hisses. 'Now leave us.' The gem is a ruby shaped like a phoenix. A rare treasure indeed, taken from a rich merchant who tried to cross the ford a long time ago. Note it on your *Adventure Sheet*. The Kappa disappear from view and you decide to move on. Turn to **335**.

362

You trudge on. The land is less cultivated here, wilder and more overgrown. Soon you are travelling between two wooded hills through a shallow valley. *Test your Luck*. If you are Lucky, turn to **386**. If you are Unlucky, turn to **396**.

363

A grisly chattering noise from the well-shaft tells you that the Rokuro-Kubi are on your tail as you grope your way blindly forward. Suddenly a slimy touch makes your face burn. Acid eats into your flesh. Lose 3 STAMINA points. If you are still alive, you shrink back in horror. The smell of brimstone is unmistakable. It is a Forsaken One – the undead soul of a wicked man who never received decent burial and whose spirit has been rejected by the spirit world because it is so twisted with malice. You must fight the Forsaken One in the pitch-blackness. Subtract 2 from your SKILL, because all you can see of it is a ghostly, glowing, yellow outline.

FORSAKEN ONE   SKILL 7   STAMINA 9

If you win, turn to **345**.

364

His eyes blaze and twin bolts of ruby light lance at you. You only just manage to avoid them. Now you must fight Gargantus, the bronze giant. Every third combat round, Gargantus fires ruby-red bolts at you from his eyes. When this occurs, roll one extra die: if it is even, you have dodged the bolts; if it is odd, you have been hit and must lose 4 STAMINA points.

GARGANTUS   SKILL 9   STAMINA 12

If you win, the Dai-Oni mutters in anger and, picking up a huge spiked iron club or tetsubo, advances towards you. Turn to **292**.

365

The first of your assailants lies dead in a pool of blood, but your own blood also stains the green turf and the peasants see that you are not invulnerable. Another attacks you, a hulking brute of a man with a wayward black beard, who is whirling a firebrand from one of the charcoal ovens round and round his head.

FIRE-WIELDER   SKILL 10   STAMINA 10

If the fire-wielder is still alive after five rounds of combat, turn to 377. If you win, turn to 389.

366

The traitor, Lord Tsietsin, is dead. The honour of the Shogun and of Hachiman has been upheld. Gain 1 Honour point for ridding the land of the evil Lord Tsietsin, and for killing him in the middle of his own castle. 'The Shogun is avenged, as are the villagers,' says Moichi, who rests, idly watching as you survey the room.

Mostly it is full of ornate decoration, but the large chest catches your interest. You quickly open it. Inside is a bag of 100 Gold Pieces, an arrow and an excellently crafted suit of Samurai armour, obviously too small for the overweight Tsietsin. You don the armour and find it is far superior to your own, especially because it is made out of some unusually light metal. Gain 1 LUCK point.

If you have the skill of Kyujutsu, you recognize the

arrow as being crafted by the legendary master of Kyujutsu, Tsunewara, who is reputed to have had magical powers. It is fletched with white eagle feathers. It should have the power of dispelling evil spirits. Note it on your *Adventure Sheet*.

Sudden sounds of shouting and the clash of weapons come from outside. Tsietsin's men will be here any minute. You both dart down the open trap-door and close it behind you. Stairs lead down into stygian blackness. You cautiously descend. Turn to **378**.

367

The trident catches a low branch and you are able to catch it and use it to threaten the Kappa. They shrink back until their yellow eyes are mere glints in the green depths. If you decide to leave now, turn to **335**. If you are determined to speak to them, turn to **361**.

368

The shattered remnants of the skeletons lie strewn about you. The undead Samurai closes in silence to do battle for the last time.

UNDEAD SAMURAI   SKILL 9   STAMINA 3

If you kill it, it falls to the ground and begins to dissolve. The sky lightens and the redness fades from the river. Among the remains of the undead Samurai you notice an ivory horn of fine workmanship, inlaid with silver tracery depicting a sabre-toothed tiger. You pick it up and walk on. Turn to **211**.

369

Your perseverance is rewarded. An improbable sight looms above you in the mist. The scarlet pagoda seems untouched by time. There are no damp stains, no rotting, the paint is immaculate. As you walk up to it, the red door swings open as if inviting you inside. If you dare to cross the threshold, turn to **299**. If you would rather return and brave the giant's causeway, turn to **113**.

370

You moan in pain, convincingly, and one of the soldiers leans over you. Suddenly you launch your attack, but you soon find you are hard pressed as you do not have your swords. The sound of battle brings more guards and they dash into the cell. One of them spears you in the chest and the blood bubbles up into your lungs. You slump to the dirty floor of the cell, to drown in your own blood.

371

The woods above Ginsei's hovel are quiet and dry. Your repose is undisturbed and you awaken much refreshed. Restore up to 3 points of lost STAMINA. As the swollen orange sun lifts the morning mists, you must decide whether to continue due north through the Longhills (turn to **237**), or to head north-west towards the villages and dales of Kanshuro (turn to **219**).

372

The Phoenix does not try to peck or claw you; instead it tries to swoop close enough to immolate itself and bathe you in flames. Each time it hits you, roll one die and subtract 1 from the result. This is the amount of STAMINA you have lost from the flames (note that you may not lose any STAMINA if you're lucky!).

PHOENIX   SKILL 9   STAMINA 7

If you win, turn to **36**.

373

The trident's tines bury themselves in your chest. If you are wearing armour, turn to **333**. If not, turn to **39**.

374

You stride up the path as if you owned the castle. The two guards flanking the doorway regard you impassively. You tell them you are ronin, a Samurai without a lord, and wish to join Tsietsin. They nod and one of them knocks on the great outer doors and steps in. Shortly, a man in a kimono steps out. 'I am Ieratsu, Lord Tsietsin's lieutenant. Please come with me.' He gestures at the door, and you step through into a large courtyard.

374

Suddenly Ieratsu shouts, 'If you are ronin, then why did you attack our men at the village? You have walked into our hands, champion of the Shogun!' A horde of warriors boil out of the castle's confines like rats and swarm over you. There are too many of them and you are overwhelmed and captured. You are unceremoniously thrown into a small cell in the palace dungeon. The gaoler, a large beefy man in a stained leather jerkin, says jeeringly, 'You will be taken before the Shogun Tsietsin on the morrow.' Then he slams the massive, iron-studded, oaken door of the cell in your face.

You are alone. They have taken your swords, and it is this rather than the cruel gibes and the indignity of capture that fills you with shame. Lose 1 Honour point for their loss. There is nothing you can do but wait for the morning, so you lie down on the wooden pallet in the corner and go to sleep. Turn to **316**.

375

As you turn to leave, the cave entrance is blocked by what appears to be an enormous moving boulder. It is in fact a Groundhog, with a body like an enormous slab of rock and eight powerful, stumpy legs. Its edges are lined with tails sporting balls of bone at their ends, like living morning stars. In the middle of its back is a huge slit-like mouth. There is nowhere to hide in the grotto; you will have to fight.

GROUNDHOG   SKILL 8   STAMINA 22

If you win, turn to **305**.

376

You follow the track leading to the castle of Lord Tsietsin. It winds through outlying farmlands, where peasants till the fields. Two sentries in ceremonial dress in the colours of Lord Tsietsin stand outside the oaken doors. As you approach, the doors swing open and a man dressed in a kimono, two swords thrust through its sash, steps out and bows.

'Welcome, welcome, champion of the Shogun. I am Ieratsu, Lord Tsietsin's lieutenant. Please step in.' As you enter the courtyard the gates shut behind you, and more than twenty armed Samurai are waiting for you. 'Unfortunately,' says Ieratsu, 'Lord Tsietsin has declared himself the new Shogun – Kihei Hasekawa is a bumbling fool, as are those who still follow him.' He signals and the soldiers charge you. Struggle as you might, there are too many of them and you are overwhelmed.

You are unceremoniously thrown into a small cell in the palace dungeon. The gaoler, a large beefy man in a stained leather jerkin, says jeeringly, 'You will be taken before the Shogun Tsietsin on the morrow.' Then he slams the massive, iron-studded, oaken door of the cell in your face.

You are alone. They have taken your swords, and it is this rather than the cruel gibes and the indignity of capture that fills you with shame. Lose 1 Honour point for their loss. There is nothing you can do but wait for the morning, so you lie down on the wooden pallet in the corner and go to sleep. Turn to **316**.

377

The battle rages on as the other charcoal-burners prepare to rain a hail of flaming torches at your head. *Test your Luck*. If you are Lucky, turn to **7**. If you are Unlucky, turn to **23**.

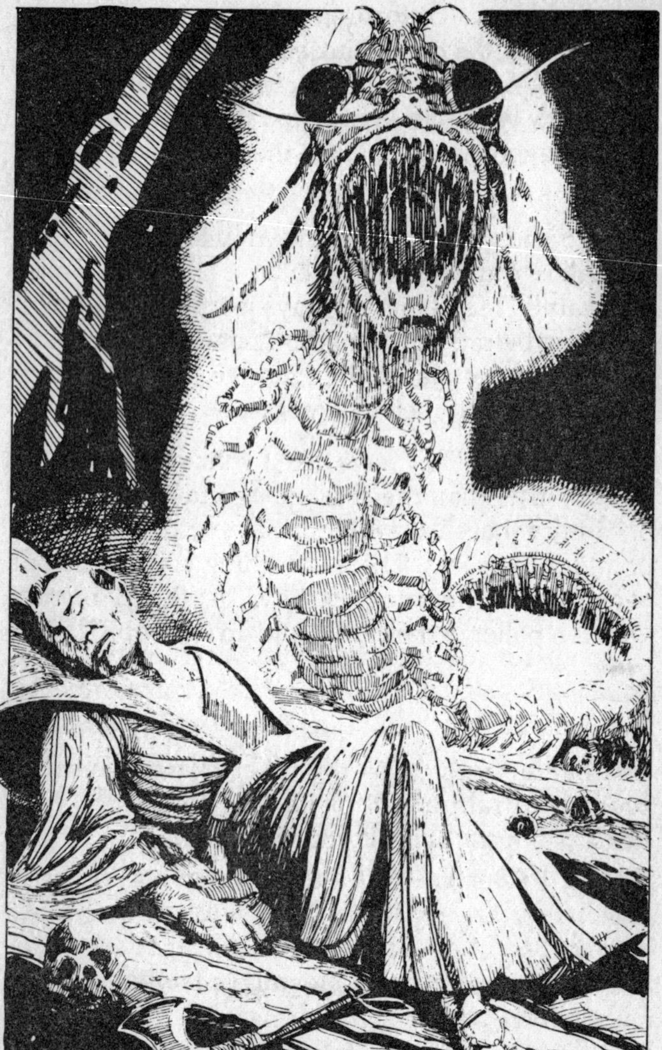

The stairs end in a blank wall. As you begin to push, it slides open. Simultaneously there is a clanging sound. Stepping through the opening, you find yourself in a damp and odorous tunnel. On the left an iron grille has slammed down, cutting you off from the stairs that climb upward beyond it. You have no choice but to follow the tunnel towards a milky-white luminescence at its end. As you and Moichi pace forward, a fetid stench rises in your nostrils.

The smell grows stronger. You come out into a large cavern, suffused with a sickly pale light, but the source of the light is for the moment indiscernible. Bones, old clothes and rusted weapons are strewn about. Then you spot it. A huge glowing shape comes towards you. An enormous gaping maw, lined with teeth rises up to devour you. Two eyes, massive discs of inscrutable blackness, stare at you, alive with ancient evil. The body, supported by hundreds of black scuttling legs, is bony and segmented. It is a dirty white colour and it is this that gives off the pale glow. It is a Mukade, some sort of gigantic, forty-foot centipede.

Moichi screams in fear and you step back in astonishment. It snaps its head forward, striking like a serpent, and bites off Moichi's arm and most of his shoulder in an instant. He moans faintly and topples to the floor.

The sight of this fills you with anger and sorrow, but

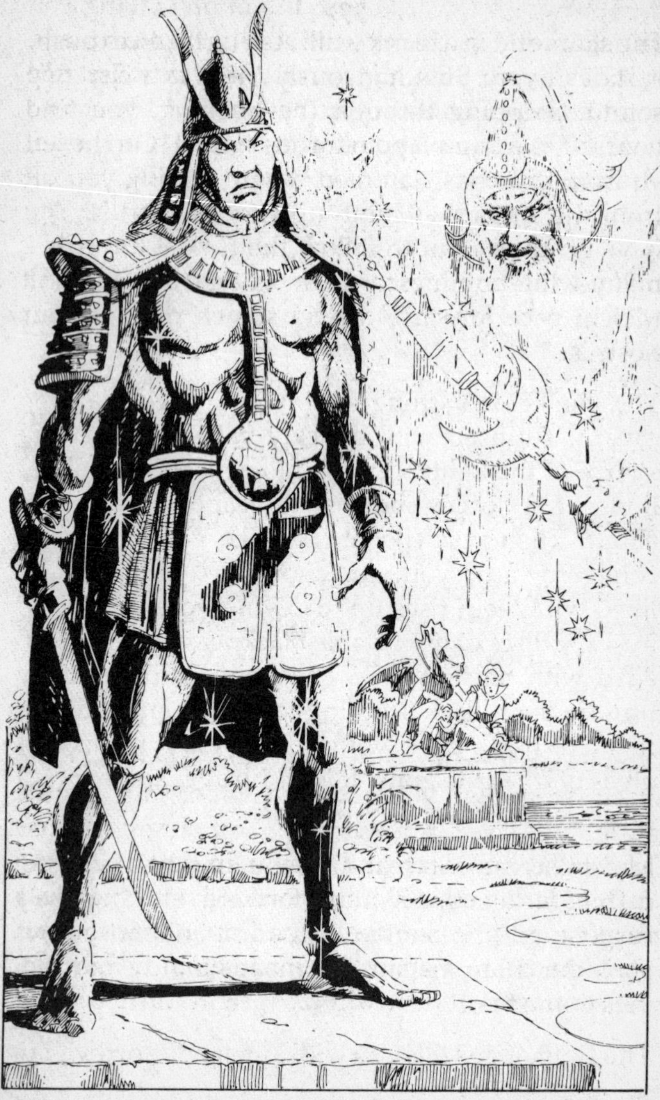

then it ripples towards you, intent on making you its next meal. If you have the skill of Kyujutsu, and still have your bow and arrow, you may fire two arrows before it is upon you. (You will not be able to reclaim the arrows if you win the fight.) In any case, you must fight it.

MUKADE   SKILL 7   STAMINA 20

If you win, turn to 384.

379
As you warily tread the path that leads to the statue of the fabled silver Samurai, the courtly magician appears at its side and sprinkles a fine blue dust over it. 'Aha, my sporting fellow, our second meeting,' he says, and he disappears in another puff of smoke. The Samurai remains chrome silver all over, but now he moves and talks. 'I challenge you, on the honour of your lord, to single combat.' Will you accept (turn to 341) or decline (turn to 321)?

380
You groan in pain. The gaoler says, 'He must have been wounded yesterday.' Two of the guards roughly lift you to your feet. You slump in their arms as if half-dead and they help you out of the cell. A darkened, cell-lined corridor stretches away to left and right. Suddenly you leap into action and grab the nearest guard's sword before he can act. Will you run left (turn to 392) or right (turn to 342)?

381

Soon you are in a low range of hills. You make fast progress until you are halted by a sheer cliff that stretches as far as the eye can see. You realize with a shock that you have mistaken your way. You must retrace your steps to the upper Hiang-Kiang River and travel on that way. After another two days you have found your way again and are ready to turn north once more. One of the tributaries of the Hiang-Kiang River lies athwart your path. The air is alive with the twittering of song-thrushes as you walk down a rolling green hillside to the river. There is a road with white-topped milestones at intervals that leads to the river and you decide to follow it. Turn to **227**.

382

The Ki-Rin flies into the air, its hoofs wreathed in flame, and arrows towards Gargantus. Gargantus looks at it and twin lancing bolts of ruby light hurtle from its eyes and hit the Ki-Rin with explosive force, killing it instantly. If you are now without allies, you will have to fight Gargantus alone. Turn to **364**. If you have Eleanor the Enchantress as your ally, turn to **22**. If you have the Golden Company as your allies, turn to **198**.

383

Inside the hovel it is surprisingly clean, though spartan. Two silk screens hang on the wall, one of Lord Toda and another showing a small village and a grand house which probably once belonged to Ginsei when he was Toda's captain: it shows two young children strongly resembling Ginsei playing below the veranda. Running your fingers over the screen to test the quality of the silk you are surprised to find a ridge in the wooden wall behind it. It proves to be a secret cupboard inside which is a black chest inlaid with letters of red gold which read 'Beware the breath of the dragon.' Will you open the chest (turn to **359**) or just take the silk screens and leave (turn to **343**)?

384

You thrust your sword deep into one of its black eyes and it rears back, uttering a shrill burbling shriek. It threshes wildly in its death-throes and you have to leap back out of the way. Presently it subsides and falls dead. Quickly you rush over to Moichi. He is still alive – but only just. Blood is oozing like the tide from the gaping wound, his face is pale and his eyes are dimming. 'At least I died with honour, my liege, and in a noble cause.' With that his spirit leaves him. You pause silently in mourning for a while, honouring his memory. But you know you must continue with your mission.

A search of the cavern reveals an exit at one end, and a heaped pile of 'treasure' – mostly bones and

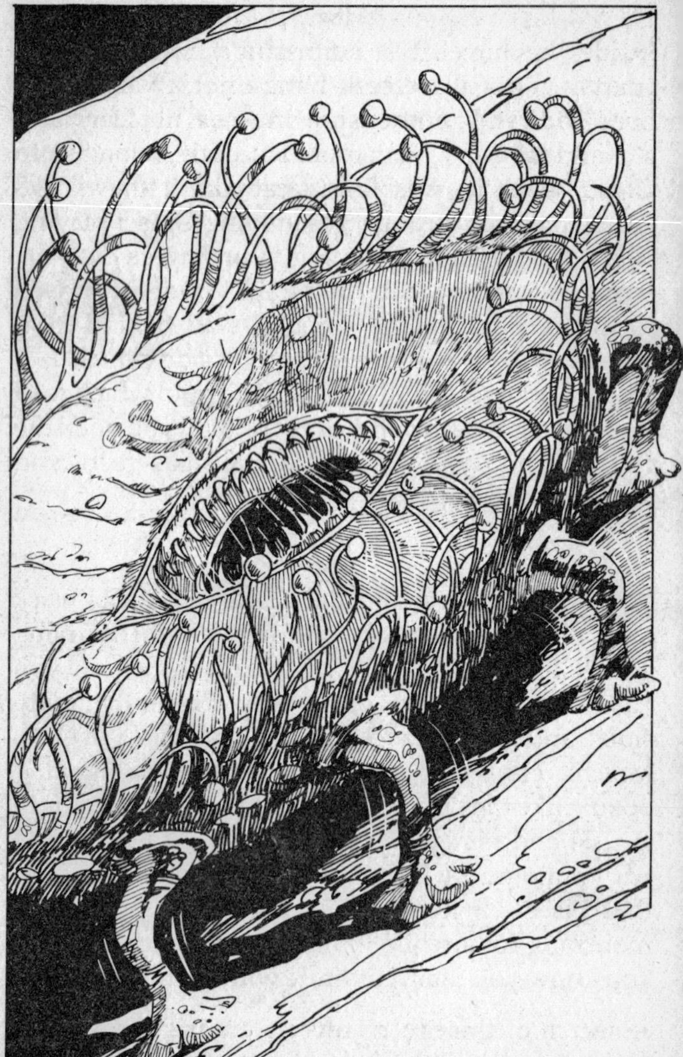

old useless weapons. However, you do find 15 Gold Pieces, a shiny silver helmet of ornate workmanship, a bottle of greenish-black ichor-like liquid and a magnificently crafted iron war-fan, used in battles to signal troops, which is inlaid with a pattern of ivory that makes you feel nauseous to look at. Will you:

Pick up the war-fan and open it?	Turn to **182**
Drink some of the liquid?	Turn to **196**
Put on the helmet?	Turn to **210**
Leave them all and go through the exit?	Turn to **222**

385

The trembling continues until the rock itself seems to curl up at the edges all around you. Too late you realize it is a Groundhog, a large monster that resembles the rock on which it lies. If you have the skill of Karumijutsu, and wish to use it, turn to **197**. If not, turn to **337**.

386

You come out of the valley and are faced by a large, forbidding forest, stretching away for miles to either side. The road disappears into its depths like a stone into water. You recognize it as the Forest of Shadows, and you must go through it. Turn to **112**.

387

Soon you come to a path that leads down to the water's edge, where a crescent of stepping-stones great columns of basalt, a veritable giant's causeway, stretches out into the mist. With difficulty you leap from one pillar to another. Turn to **113**.

388

You stealthily circle the castle, without being seen. Then you dart forward to beneath its walls, which you find are made of fine, well-dressed, stone blocks, and you cannot find any footholds for climbing. However, if you have the skill of Karumijutsu, you may be able to reach the battlements. If you wish to try this, turn to **284**. If not, you can approach the gate and try to bluff your way in (turn to **374**), abandon the attempt to slay Tsietsin and press on (turn to **338**), or wait near the entrance and hope some opportunity to get in arises (turn to **398**).

389

Your prowess with the katana has instilled terror in the hearts of the charcoal-burners. The fire-wielder's body lies horribly contorted before you and the others scatter and flee into the woods. You have defended the honour of your lord and you may add 1 to your own Honour score before continuing on your way. Turn to **195**.

390

You dash back, wrench the door open and dive through. The Phoenix does not attempt to prevent you. You are back in the Hub, surrounded by stars and the eight doors. Return to **8** and choose again, but you cannot choose an option you have chosen once already.

391

The magnificent beast shakes the very earth as it falls. Part of its ebony antlers was shorn off by your blade. The Black Elk weighs several tons and it is far too large to skin quickly, but you may cut some meat from the still warm carcass. Add 2 to your Provisions. The broken piece of antler is adorned by a strange whorled pattern, almost like a serpent of white bone. You decide to keep the antler as a talisman. Note it on your *Adventure Sheet* and turn to **381**.

392

You spring away before the guards have reacted, such is their surprise. You have one sword, at least. Until you get another you cannot use the skill of Ni-to-Kenjutsu, nor can you use Kyujutsu until you obtain a bow and arrows, if you chose either of these skills during your training.

The corridor ends in a stairwell, going both up and down. The guards are catching up. Will you go up (turn to **18**) or down (turn to **4**)?

393

The Kappa, for that is what the scaly green monsters are, glare balefully at you, their yellow eyes just below the surface. Legends tell that they are wily and capable of speaking in the human tongue. Will you leave immediately, while it is possible to do so (turn to **335**), or try to talk to them (turn to **325**)?

394

The Ki-Rin flies up and circles the Dai-Oni. The Dai-Oni swings the club at it, but the Ki-Rin dodges aside. Then the Ki-Rin utters a single word and the Dai-Oni screams in pain. 'You have stripped me of my magic, cursed beast!' he screams. The Ki-Rin flies up, saying, 'That is all I can do, mortal: the rest is in your hands. Good luck.' Then it fades from view. The Dai-Oni advances, club in hand, but this time you can see fear in its eyes. You must fight it.

DAI-ONI   SKILL 10   STAMINA 10

If you win, turn to **54**.

395

You clamber on to a mossy mound near the far bank of the river, as several scaly green monsters rise dripping from the depths and converge upon you. If you have the skill of Karumijutsu and wish to try to leap over their heads to safety, turn to **35**. If you decide to stand your ground and fight it out, turn to **13**. If, instead, you surrender, turn to **3**.

396

A troop of fifteen riders appears on the road ahead of you. They are wearing blue and green lacquered battle armour and you recognize the symbol emblazoned on a banner one of them bears: they are Samurai of Lord Tsietsin. The leading Samurai hails you, saying, 'Welcome to the domain of Lord Tsietsin. You are the Shogun's champion, are you not?' You nod as they approach, smiling.

Suddenly one of them shouts, 'And Lord Tsietsin has declared himself the new Shogun!' With that they charge you, taking you by surprise. You struggle mightily, slaying three of them and wounding several more, but there are too many and soon you are securely bound and strapped over a horse's back. 'Lord Tsietsin will be pleased with this little catch,' one of them quips.

They take you to the castle you passed on the road. You are led into the courtyard, where many of Lord Tsietsin's Samurai retainers gather around to laugh and mock you. You are unceremoniously thrown into a small cell in the palace dungeon. The gaoler, a

396

large beefy man in a stained leather jerkin, says jeeringly, 'You will be taken before the Shogun Tsietsin on the morrow.' Then he slams the massive, iron-studded, oaken door of the cell in your face.

You are alone. They have taken your swords, and it is this rather than the cruel gibes and the indignity of capture that fills you with shame. Lose 1 Honour point for their loss. There is nothing you can do but wait for the morning, so you lie down on the wooden pallet in the corner and go to sleep. Turn to **316**.

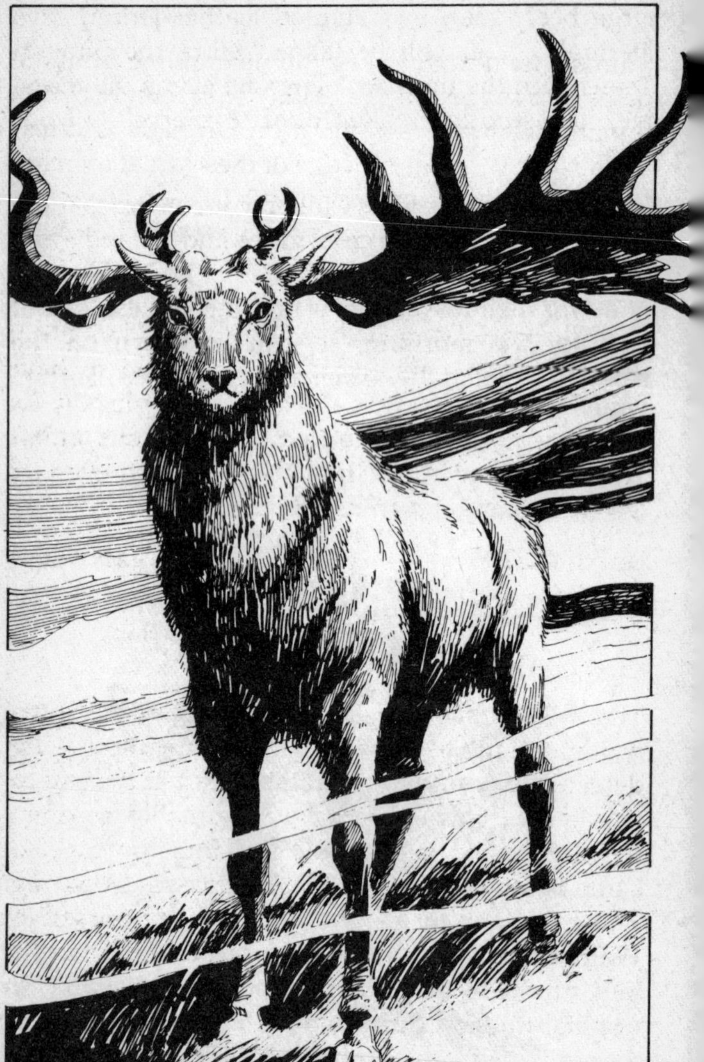

397

Sunrise the next day sees you descending from the dales into the last of the lands held securely by the Shogun. Gaunt trees litter a brown plain and tear the mist. You rest at the edge of these drear marcher lands before going on. Restore up to 4 lost STAMINA points. On the following day you stride out through the mist – which muffles the sound of heavy hoofbeats until they are almost upon you. A great black beast looms over you in the mist. It is the Black Elk of the Marcher Lands, which is supposed to have vanished seventy years ago or more. Unluckily for you it seems to have returned. Its enormous antlers are fifteen feet of polished ebony and its eyes are jewels of flame. You must fight.

BLACK ELK   SKILL 9   STAMINA 18

If you win, turn to **391**.

398

You wait at some distance from the castle gates, trying to think of some way to get in without being detected. Presently you notice a cart trundling towards you, laden with hay, presumably making a delivery to the castle. You dart into the cover of some nearby undergrowth and it passes slowly by. There is plenty of hay for you to hide yourself in. Will you creep up behind the cart and hide in the hay (turn to **6**), abandon this and press on with your original mission (turn to **338**), or try to bluff your way in through the gates (turn to **374**)?

399

Ginsei lies dead at your feet, his lacquered blue armour rent and stained purple. He will never dishonour the name of the Shogun again. Smoke still rises from the hovel in which he had been hiding out. Will you investigate the hut (turn to 383), or find a dry spot to sleep in the woods (turn to 371)?

400

The black robes that encased the Master of Shadows fall to the floor in a heap. Ikiru is no more. The walls of his dark hall begin to shudder and his throne to crumble. The pit falls in on itself. Great cracks appear in the floor. Desperately you search for an entrance, but then part of a wall falls away and clean sunlight passes in. Wincing from the glare, you run out to find yourself in the Shios'ii Mountains. Behind you the great black palace of strange, alien design is crumbling away, the palace of Ikiru.

You find yourself in the midst of a camp of Shikome, but they are ignoring you. Some of them are staring in horrified fear at the palace, others are running hither and thither in panic. You take this opportunity to leave quickly and you escape unmolested.

A few days later, you are safely back in Konichi, the capital, where the Shogun holds a state banquet in your honour. With the return of Singing Death, his rule is assured and the Lords of Hachiman unite under his banner, to repel the barbarian invaders. With Ikiru slain, his army of Shikome disperse and the threat is lifted. An age of peace and prosperity lies ahead of you and the people of Hachiman.